Namibia: SWAPO Fights For Freedom

**PLAN militants march
to attack enemy forces
inside Namibia - MPLA photo**

DT
714
N354

Published and Printed by
LSM Information Center
P.O. Box 2077
Oakland, CA 94604 USA

©1978 by LSM Information Center. All rights reserved.

First Printing — 1978
Library of Congress Catalog Card Number: 78-50386
International Standard Book Number: 0-919914-27-6
Printed in USA

Table
Of
Contents

Preface

Much of the material in this book was published in a double issue of *LSM NEWS* (No. 11-12) in October 1976. As that issue sold out, however, demand for documentation on SWAPO and the Namibian liberation struggle kept growing. We have removed some dated material from the first version and added fresh documentation. The Introduction, too, is written especially for this book.

Like all LSM literature, this book's purpose is to raise the political consciousness of our readers. We strive for critical analysis and objectivity—not to be confused with neutrality. We have tried to present the issue of Namibian liberation as clearly as possible in the belief that those who understand what is at stake in Namibia will support the liberation struggle.

We also aim to stimulate practical anti-imperialist action. In the back of the book you will find suggestions for effective action, as well as the addresses of some organizations that work in support of SWAPO. Now that the United States and other Western governments are trying to force a neocolonial option on the Namibian liberation struggle, our role must be to support those who fight for genuine economic, political and cultural liberation.

ONE NAMIBIA, ONE NATION!
SWAPO WILL WIN!

Liberation Support Movement

Namibia

Cunene River
Pereira de Eça
Angola
Ruacana
Okavango River
Okalongo •Oshikango
Ohopoho• •Ondangua
Runtu
OVAMBOLAND
Caprivi Strip

Namutoni
Tsumeb
•Grootfontein
Outo•
Otjiwarongo

Omaruru
Usakos •Okahandja
Swakopmund Windhoek• •Gobabis

Walvis Bay
Rehoboth

Mariental

Atlantic
Ocean
Luderitz
Keetmanshoop

Botswana

South

Oranjemund Orange River

Africa

Zambia
Angola Zambezi R
Katima Mulilo
Caprivi Strip

Introduction

"Economic reconstruction in a free, democratic, and united Namibia will have as its motive force the establishment of a classless society. Social justice and progress for all is the governing idea behind every SWAPO policy decision."

These words—from the Political Program of the South West Africa People's Organization (SWAPO of Namibia)—mean a great deal to millions across the world who fight against an oppressive system which we identify in many ways and places as imperialism. These words suggest the building of a new type of society where human beings, and not profits, are our central concern. Current developments in Southern Africa show that such notions are not idle dreams of an "idealistic" few but are daily becoming realities in such countries as Angola and Mozambique, just as they invigorate the liberation struggles of neighboring Zimbabwe and South Africa, as well.

Southern Africa today is the stage for one of the greatest dramas of our era. Since World War II, colonized and oppressed peoples throughout the world have been rising to recapture their freedom. Some of their struggles have succeeded; many have stopped halfway. But their efforts have provided a wealth of experience from which Namibians, Zimbabweans and South Africans can benefit as their nations move to the center of this historic conflict. Their respective strategies for the liberation struggle are determined by the specific conditions of each country. Underlying the particulars of each situation, however, is a basic lesson of decolonization: Only with the active participation of the masses of people and only with a thorough restructuring of the country's economy can national liberation fulfill its promises. Without these ingredients, the dependence, domination and oppression of the colonial period remain unassailable. The above statement from SWAPO's political program tells us that the Namibian liberation movement, as it gains strength in every field, has accepted this fundamental challenge.

Namibia (called South West Africa by European colonizers) stretches from the western reaches of the Kalahari Desert to the Atlantic Ocean. The central part of the country rests on a high plateau where vegetation is good for sheep and cattle grazing. The low-lying northern part of the country supports crop cultivation. The desolate Namib Desert, from which the country derives its name, makes up almost the entire coastline—called the "Skeleton Coast" by early European seafarers.

From time immemorial Namibia has been inhabited by the San ("Bushmen") whose ancient rock paintings tell the story of this people's early hunting and gathering existence. These same paintings also portray the arrival of other peoples with their herds of cattle; first the Nama and Damara, later the Herero and the Ovambo. The Ovambos settled in the vicinity of the Cunene River (today northern Namibia and southern Angola). By the end of the sixteenth century, these five peoples had learned to coexist and limit their periodic feuds and friction so that the overall balance between them was not upset. The Ovambos were thrifty cultivators who grew a variety of cereals and raised some cattle; the Hereros and Namas kept far bigger herds, and the Damaras worked as herdspeople for both the Namas and Hereros.

The first pressure from European colonization made itself felt in the early nineteenth century when another group of Namas arrived from the South, driven away by white settlement in the Cape. Some years later followed a group of Basters—people of mixed African-Dutch ancestry. Many among these two groups were Christians and brought with them such European technology as firearms.

Delayed by the hostile Namib Desert and the arid expanses to the north of the Cape, the Europeans themselves did not arrive for another few decades. Finally, in the 1860's traders and missionaries became a frequent sight in the land of the Hereros and Namas, and in 1878, the Cape Colony government annexed Walvis Bay, the only suitable deep-water port on the Namib coast. Twenty-five years later, by a familiar pattern of bribery, deceit and outright genocide, the Nama and Herero peoples had been militarily conquered, driven from the best of their lands, and reduced to one-third of their pre-colonial population level.

The colonization of Namibia stands out among the bloodiest undertakings in Africa's history. For reasons European, not African, Bismarck's Germany took this part of the continent at the 1884-85 Berlin Conference and set out to carry on with the conquest begun the year before. European power prevailed with a vengeance and the bloodbath went far beyond the German need to gain military control. In 1904, after the decisive battle of the German-Herero War, the German commander issued the following "Extermination Order":

Within the German boundaries, every Herero, whether found

armed or unarmed, with or without cattle, will be shot—I shall not accept any more women and children. I shall drive them back. ... These are my words to the Herero people. Signed: Great General of the Mighty Kaiser, von Trotha.[1]

Apart from military inferiority, the inability of the African peoples to unite when faced with the white colonizer precipitated their defeat and decimation. Economically and politically subjugated, it was to take them half a century to again mount an effective challenge to white power.

The Germans managed to penetrate only the southern three-quarters of their colony. In 1915, during World War I, they were driven from the country by a force of 43,000 white South African volunteers who promised freedom to the Africans, won their collaboration—and then proceeded to take the rest of the territory, the land of the Ovambos.

At the end of the world war, the South Africans certainly expected to be allowed to annex "German" South West Africa as a reward for their effort. When, under pressure from US President Wilson, they finally agreed to merely administer the country "in the interest of the indigenous population," their concession was mainly semantic. They knew that the League of Nations "would consist mostly of the same people who were present [at Versailles], who understood the [South African] position, and who would not make it impossible . . . to govern the country."[2] The Namibians were not consulted as their country, the noble words of the Covenant notwithstanding, was once more sold into bondage. In reality, the document signed in Versailles in 1920 represented their interests no more than did the one signed thirty-five years earlier in Berlin.

South African colonization was far more thorough than that of the Germans. Afrikaner settlers, police, and administrators came trekking in from the South. Africans were enclosed in barren reserves from which they could only escape as dirt-cheap laborers for the white-owned farms and industry. Anti-colonial resistance was ruthlessly crushed, as in 1932 when the South African air force bombed the quarters of a rebel chief.

In the late 1940's two events occurred which came to shape the contemporary struggle for Namibia. First, the newly formed United Nations in 1946 rejected the legitimacy of South Africa's *de facto* colonization of Namibia and thus opened a long and well-documented legal battle. This futile effort to give Namibia independence by peaceful means reached a highpoint in 1966 when the UN General Assembly terminated the 1920 League of Nations mandate and again in 1971 when the World Court "obliged" South Africa to "withdraw its administration from Namibia immediately." Second, the 1948 election victory of the Afrikaner Nationalists in South Africa ushered in the apartheid system. White racial superiority became law and the black people of both South Africa and Namibia were assigned to do nothing else but produce wealth for the ruling minority. As the apartheid regime violently consolidated its power, it closed off every option but counter-violence for the Namibian people to gain their freedom.

Apartheid is firmly rooted in the economic needs of the South African ruling minority. This holds true in South Africa as much as in Namibia where this vicious system dates back to the initial period of occupation. Even before World War I ended, the new colonial regime established a labor recruitment system that drew the strongest and healthiest African men off the reserves to work in the mines and farms in the "Police (White) Zone." Within this zone, which comprises almost three-quarters of the entire country, only Africans with a "pass" can legally live, Africans traveling from one place to another still require government permission, and no African can own livestock or land.

Over the decades, reserve boundaries and restrictions on African economic activity have been shaped to meet the growing demands of the colonial economy. By 1962 the 73,000 Whites in the country owned 48% of the land while the 430,000 rural Africans had 25%. Because of the inferior quality of the African land, however, even this grim statistic is misleading. For instance, only half of relatively crowded Ovamboland can be used for cattle grazing, and 40% of the recorded population live in 7% of the "homeland" area. As a result, the Ovambos have 9.6 hectares of useful land per person as compared to 1,625 hectares for rural Whites. In other words, Whites depending on farming have *170 times more useful land* than the average Ovambo! A British engineer who visited the region in 1973 (one of the few foreigners permitted to do so) reported that "although Ovamboland is a relatively fertile part of the country, I saw for myself how it is being turned into a dustbowl by overgrazing. A serious drought can mean famine for the inhabitants, yet Namibia is one of the richest countries in Africa in terms of GNP per capita!"[3]

We see therefore in Namibia—as in all colonial and neocolonial countries—not *one* national economy but *two*: the miserable subsistence economy which cannot sustain the African population even at the most basic level of human existence and the booming export-oriented economy run by the Whites. Many Africans have been integrated into the latter, which in turn has become completely dependent on their slave-wage level and captive labor for its functioning. In 1967 the average per capita income for Whites in Namibia was estimated at $2,242, *twenty-six times more* than the $85.40 estimated for Africans in the reserves![4]

The three main sectors of the colonial economy are mining, fishing, and agriculture. All three depend heavily on "contract" labor from the reserves. Until the big contract workers' strike of 1971–72 crippled Namibian industry for several months, this labor was supplied by the South West African Native Labour Association (SWANLA) which each year supplied tens of thousands of Namibian men to farms, mines, and factories throughout the Police Zone. The men were classified as "A," "B," or "C" depending on their experience and physical condition, given a tag with their classification and their employer's name to wear round their neck, and shipped off for twelve or eighteen months. During the period of the contract, it was a criminal offense for the worker to quit his job or even leave the area of his work. His family, of course, had to stay behind in the reserve. Before the 1971 strike, the wages for contract workers varied from (US) $5.25 to $14.70 *per month*. Many employers paid out the wages only at the end of the contract period to ensure that the workers did not "escape."

One can imagine the disastrous social effects of such a system on the African population. With 25% or more of the adult male population away on contract at any one time, community life is broken up and families dislocated. The workers themselves live penned up in huge "compounds" where their loneliness and frustration can find few outlets. If the worker has a large family to support, three or four months at home may be all he can afford before going out on the next contract. So deep runs the workers' antagonism toward the contract that they demanded its complete abolition when they struck in 1971.

Following the strike, the regime announced reforms, including wage increases. These, however, did little to change the system if we are to believe the report in the Johannesburg *Financial Times* from a meeting of Windhoek's Master Builders' Association:

Sipping lagerbier and scotch, delegates rejected (some vociferously) a suggestion that a minimum hourly wage of [21 US cents] be paid to unskilled laborers in the building industry. . . . Eventually delegates agreed that the minimum recommended starting wage would be [10 US cents] an hour. This is exactly one third of the . . . minimum for unskilled African laborers in

Transvaal [South Africa].[5]

Profiting from Namibian slave labor and hiding behind the virtual information blackout of the South African government are many US corporations. The largest private employer in the country is the American Metal Climax (AMAX) owned and run Tsumeb Corporation which since 1947 has brought incredible profits to its US owners and by 1969 paid $140 million in taxes to the South African government. That is probably four or five times as much as it paid in wages to its Namibian workers (5,000 in 1970) whose average wage in 1973 was $54 per month. Average wages for Whites were *Thirteen times* higher.

Like AMAX, many other American corporations are pillars of colonialism in Namibia. They include Newmont Mining Corporation, US Steel, Bethlehem Steel, Phelps Dodge, and the Del Monte Corporation, which imports into the US large quantities of fish from a Walvis Bay cannery. Together with South African, British, French, Canadian, and West German corporations, they are doing what they can to pump out the natural riches of Namibia while they still have a free reign. The country's fabulous diamond deposits may only last another fifteen years and the rich fishing grounds off the coast even less. Only then, when the country's wealth has been exhausted like the worn-out contract worker who returns almost penniless to the "homeland" from his last term, will these exploiters consider modifying the terms of their presence in Namibia.

No African or "Colored" bourgeoisie has emerged from the colonial exploitation of Namibia. The big farms of the Police Zone, the mines, and the other industry are all owned and run by settlers or by foreign interests, and Africans are by law excluded from owning property outside the reserves. Within the reserves the South African regime has for a pittance bought the loyalty of a few tribal chiefs whose role it is to give a semblance of legitimacy to the South African occupation of Namibia. These chiefs are dependent on the colonial government and have little wealth and power on their own—despite South African efforts to build them up.

The great majority of Namibians are forced to carve out a living as best they can from the sandy and eroding soil of the reserves. Many of these peasants, particularly among the Ovambos, have been integrated into the colonial economy by "exporting" the best of their labor. The others, such as the San and the Caprivians, still live largely within their traditional ways, but are fighting a losing battle against capitalist intrusion. Neither group has received anything in return for the expropriation of their land and labor power. The

14

handful of schools outside the Police Zone are run by missionaries while medical care and modern technology have been completely absent. Only during the past decade, under pressure from the liberation struggle and international protest, has the South African government tried to paint a brighter facade by building a few schools and clinics.

Approximately one-fifth of the African population live outside the reserves, mainly in the "townships" or "locations" that surround the white towns of the Police Zone. These people serve as a permanent labor force for the colonial economy. Some work as domestic servants, others in factories and the building industry, doing the skilled or semi-skilled tasks one step above the contract laborers. Many are absorbed as clerks, drivers, cleaners, etc., in the service industries of larger towns such as Windhoek and Walvis Bay. On the top rung of the African ladder are those few "semi-professionals" who work as teachers or office personnel and those who own shops within the locations. The wage level of all these urban Africans is higher than that of the contract workers, and social services are more easily accessible than in the reserves.

Of these groups it was among the urban workers and "petty bourgeoisie" that the contemporary liberation movement first took hold. Their day-to-day contact with the white rulers and some knowledge of the outside world—particularly the anti-apartheid resistance movement within South Africa—produced in the late 1950's the first activities aimed at ending the South African occupation. The second major group to join the struggle was the contract workers who in the early 1960's were becoming politicized through the work of SWAPO organizers. Their migration back and forth from the Police Zone to the "homelands" spread the idea of independence throughout the country. Ovamboland, where Angolan guerrillas were fighting Portuguese colonialism just across the border, became a particularly active pocket of political mobilization. A third group to join en masse was the school youth, thousands of teenagers who in the early 1970's closed down schools and staged open demonstrations against the South African regime.

Today, all segments of the Namibian population take part in the national liberation struggle; SWAPO mobilization and South African repression have left no corner of the country untouched. Despite the efforts of the regime and its hand-picked collaborators, tribalism and ethnic divisions are giving way to a national consciousness. In 1976 and 1977 alone, more than a dozen tribally based organizations dissolved to join SWAPO. This growing national unity, across ethnic, class and religious divisions, has now become a major obstacle to continued South African domination of the country.

In this book we have put together a variety of documents on SWAPO and the struggle in Namibia to convey some of the perspectives and experiences of people who have dedicated their lives to making revolution. Many people have expressed an interest in knowing more about SWAPO: how do they fight; what problems do they face; what is their history? In the opening interview, SWAPO President Sam Nujoma discusses the history of the liberation movement and conveys SWAPO's main considerations for an independent Namibia. In a rare interview with a SWAPO military cadre, Kakauru Nganjone of the People's Liberation Army of Namibia (PLAN) shows that not all the problems of waging a people's war are military—that in fact, political considerations are primary in SWAPO's efforts.

The process of genuine national liberation must encompass a parallel struggle for the liberation of women. The oppression and exploitation of African women are rooted in both the traditional and the colonial heritage. The struggle for women's emancipation is therefore a difficult one, and often more subtle than the fight against the colonial oppressor. In "The Women Militants" two female SWAPO members place the situation of Namibian women within the national liberation struggle and take a frank look at some of the hurdles that have yet to be cleared.

"The Price of Liberation" is a slice of the life story of Hinananje Nehova, one of the young militants who joined SWAPO in the surge of the early 1970's and went on to help organize the great contract workers' strike before being captured by the South African police. His story, as well as the "Letter from Robben Island" which follows it, is dedicated to those hundreds of Namibian political prisoners who today are held under the most brutal conditions in the jails of the South African regime.

The final section of the book is made up of recent SWAPO political documents, including the movement's current program. Together, these documents show how the struggle against colonial rule by necessity is also a struggle against imperialism and for socialism.

The liberation of Namibia is part of the liberation of the entire Southern African subcontinent. The future of the country is inextricably linked to the struggles for liberation in South Africa and Zimbabwe and to the consolidation of independence and building of socialism in Angola and Mozambique.

In the past four years, starting with the collapse of Portuguese colonialism in 1974, a number of important setbacks have hit South Africa, the Rhodesian settler regime, and their supporters in North America and Western Europe. Their dismal failure to prevent MPLA from taking power in Angola, the fiasco of the South African invasion of that country, the explosive revolt of South Africa's urban Blacks, the ability of the Frelimo government to establish itself firmly throughout Mozambique, the surge of armed liberation struggle in Zimbabwe—all these events represent a tremendous setback to imperialist interests. In Namibia the results have been a great advance in the armed struggle and a new wave of open support for SWAPO from all corners of the country.

But imperialism has rapidly adapted its approach to the new reality and is now launching its counter-offensive. At stake is the ultimate survival of capitalist domination in Southern Africa, whether in its present extreme racist form or with some modification. The South African regime sees its own survival linked to a "stable" Namibia and has, since its 1976 defeat in Angola, turned northern Namibia into a vast military base. 50,000 South African troops now enforce absolute control over the Namibian people, thousands of whom have been herded into so-called strategic hamlets. In the North, villages have been destroyed, crops burned, and livestock slaughtered where the all-white colonial troops have created their "free-fire zones."

South African troops are not the only soldiers here. Israeli counter-insurgency experts have assisted in anti-guerrilla operations, and SWAPO has reported that even Chilean troops have now arrived to gain experience in this type of war! Angolan anti-communist exiles of FNLA and UNITA are trained and equipped in northern Namibia between military actions against the Angolan government and villagers. South African troops at times join the raids into Angola, intent on keeping the Angolan revolution on the defensive.

But the government in Pretoria, too, knows that the battle for Namibia will not be determined by force alone. It is therefore busy preparing a political "solution" that its Western allies will find acceptable, and which at the same time will allow South Africa to dominate its colony indefinitely. The regime is preparing to divide Namibia into thirteen tribally based and chief-ruled "bantustans" which will form a federation. The white population will continue to dominate the country, particularly since "independence" is not likely to affect control of industry and distribution of land in any major way. Each tribal mini-state will have its own army—forces which are already being trained to fight against SWAPO. This plan, says SWAPO President Nujoma, "is intended to set the stage for a civil war in Namibia, thereby providing a pretext for Pretoria to re-occupy Namibia even after independence."

The "independence" that we can soon expect to see written up in the North American press—as a gesture of good will on the part of South Africa—will be one of isolated, barren "homelands," incapable of economic self-sufficiency, and controlled by the apartheid regime. In the meantime, SWAPO concludes, "the multi-national corporations will continue to exploit Namibian mineral wealth while the Namibians continue to suffer from hunger, disease and ignorance."[6] It would be the repeat of an already too familiar scenario in "post-colonial" Africa.

Though South Africa's Western allies may feel embarrassed or even indignant about the cruder aspects of apartheid, their main concern is to blunt the radicalizing effect of the liberation struggle on the Namibians. Five of these powers have therefore taken it upon themselves to act as go-betweens for SWAPO and the South African government. It is no accident that these five—the United States, Britain, France, Canada, and West Germany—are also the home base for most of the giant corporations which rob Namibia of its wealth. Their intentions are clear enough. "They are really talking with their ally [South Africa] to find . . . how a regime could be established that would protect their interests," a SWAPO official commented.[7]

The US on its own went a step further to prepare for the future. In 1977 the State Department commissioned a preliminary study on how the US could quickly come to the "aid" of independent Namibia. One aspect of the envisaged American assistance was the training and equipping of a new Namibian army—presumably not the SWAPO guerrilla army.

Despite this many-sided imperialist counter-attack, time is not on their side. Their efforts to isolate and "destabilize" Angola have not succeeded, and that country remains an important rear base for the SWAPO guerrillas who now operate far into the Police Zone. At the same time, intimidation, imprisonment, and executions do not appear to have reduced the liberation movement's strength among the great majority of Namibians. Some time ago SWAPO established conditions for negotiating with the South Africans.* Many SWAPO militants believe that the intensification of the armed liberation war will ultimately force their enemy to accept those conditions.

But it would be foolhardy to ignore the huge barriers that remain

18

before SWAPO's stated goals can be achieved. If the pressures for neocolonial accommodation are strong today, they will double after liberation. Namibia's complete dependence on South Africa for many of its essential supplies cannot be eliminated overnight. In the same vein, it will take time to train cadres to run mines and industries, to improve food production, and to create decent social services for all the people. The transitional period will be one of many hardships which will thoroughly test the new government's strength.

It is therefore necessary to look ahead. We must live with the outcome of the present struggle in Southern Africa for many years to come. It will profoundly influence economic and political life within all capitalist countries. A setback for capitalism in that part of the world will be yet another step in the process of its global disintegration. This process is not automatic; it demands action. And for this action responsibility also lies with those North Americans who want an end to capitalist exploitation. It is on this level that our solidarity with the Namibian people begins.

February, 1978
Liberation Support Movement

---

* SWAPO's conditions can be summarized as follows:

    a) South Africa withdraws all its armed forces from Namibia;

    b) South Africa releases all Namibian political prisoners;

    c) South Africa respects Namibia's territorial integrity, including Walvis Bay;

    d) South Africa and the five Western countries of the so-called contact group recognize the UN Council of Namibia as the only legal authority over the country.

NOTES

1. Quoted in Randolph Vigne, *A Dwelling Place of Our Own*, (London 1973), p. 12.
2. Ibid., p. 15
3. Peter Fraenkel, *The Namibians of South-West Africa*, (London 1974), p. 32.
4. W. Courtney and J. Davis, *Namibia: U.S. Corporate Involvement*, (New York 1972), p. 10
5. Quoted in ibid., p. 12.
6. Both quotes are from an interview with President Sam Nujoma in *Southern Africa* (New York), November 1977, p. 21.
7. SWAPO Central Committee member and UN Representative Theo-Ben Gurirab in *New African Development* (London), October 1977, p. 982.

ONE NAMIBIA, ONE NATION!

Twenty
Years
Of
Struggle

drawing by
Selma Waldman

21

Comrade Nujoma, could you tell us about your own background and how you came to be involved in the Namibian nationalist movement?

I was born on May 12, 1929 in the northern region of Namibia at the village called Onganjera. Like all the boys of those days, I used to look after my father's cattle, goats and sheep. I attended a Finnish missionary school, where at that time we were only taught in the Ovambo language and the subjects were based on the Bible. My parents wanted me to become a priest. After World War II, I went to Windhoek to live with my uncle and to attend St. Barnabas English School. But before I completed my studies, the South African government took over and imposed "Bantu education." You see, Bantu education is simply brain-washing the African to believe that he's inferior to the White—to prepare him for a life of laboring for the white "baas." Many students, including myself, left school and took up correspondence studies instead.

By this time I had to support myself, so I went to work for the South African Railways. I worked under the typical Afrikaaners, or Boers, who are very arrogant and show an open hatred of Blacks. While working for the railroad, I began to understand the true character of the oppressive, racist South African regime. For instance, I saw many serious injuries where a worker would lose an arm or a leg, then would be sent back to the reserve with no compensation whatsoever, no longer able to make a living.

I saw this oppression with my own eyes and I experienced it myself; right then I decided to do something about it. As other Namibians were doing at this time, I began to write petitions to the United Nations. The only response would be a reply like, "We received your letter dated such and such and we have taken note of it." Nothing beyond that. Meanwhile, our oppression continued.

My fellow workers and I began to realize the need for an organization which would give us a forceful voice to raise our demands for self-determination. In April 1959 we met in Windhoek and formed the Ovamboland People's Organization (OPO). At this first OPO Congress I was elected President. Again next year when the organization became the South West Africa People's Organization (SWAPO), I was elected President of the Movement and have remained so up to this day.

In 1959 we began organizing sit-ins and demonstrations which the South Africans considered illegal. I was repeatedly arrested and tried. Even though my cases were usually dismissed by the court magistrate, SWAPO was spending a lot of time and money on my defense. So it was decided that I could be more effective outside the country by representing our people at the UN. I left Namibia in March 1960, escaping through Botswana, Rhodesia and Zambia to Tanzania. There I was helped by Nyerere, who is now the President of Tanzania, and traveled to New York, where I presented the Namibian people's just cause for freedom and independence to the UN. In January 1961, I returned to Africa and opened an office in Tanzania, which was then approaching independence, and SWAPO began to operate from outside the country.

Your first organization, the OPO, was formed largely by Ovambo workers and later became a national party which in the beginning used non-violent methods of struggle. Perhaps you could discuss the developments which changed SWAPO into a national liberation movement leading an armed struggle for independence.

Well, during the 1950's many Namibians went to South Africa where they worked on contract, mostly in the mines. A large number of them went to Cape Town where they came in contact with the African National Congress (ANC) of South Africa and other parties opposed to white minority rule. These colleagues learned about the struggles in South Africa; they knew also that we were petitioning the UN and demanding our legitimate rights of self-determination and independence. So, like us, they came to recognize the need for an organization which could represent the aspirations of our people. Because the majority of them were Ovambos, which is the largest and most oppressed group of people under the contract system, they drew up a constitution to form the OPO to fight this contract system. Those of us in Windhoek received a copy of this constitution. After studying it, we fully agreed with this organization's aims and objectives and founded the OPO on April 15, 1959. However, the name did not characterize the national aspirations of the Namibian people as a whole, and so in early 1960 it was changed to the South West Africa People's Organization.

Within six months of SWAPO's formation we had made a tremendous impact by our mass mobilizing campaigns. We demanded the abolition of racial discrimination and the contract system, the right of Namibians to express themselves freely and the end of the South African colonial administration.

One of our first actions was a boycott of beer halls, cinemas and buses to protest the removal of Africans from a traditional residential area in Windhoek. According to South African apartheid policy, the African location was too close to the white residential area and had to be demolished. We organized a peaceful demonstration, but

23

the South African police opened fire on the people, killing more than twelve on the spot and injuring more than fifty. The brutal repressive policy of the South Africans caught us by surprise. We had thought that we should carry on our struggle with the peaceful methods used elsewhere in Africa. But our demonstrations, boycotts and strikes were met with brute force and many leaders of SWAPO were tortured and killed.

At the same time our peaceful efforts on the diplomatic front were frustrated by the inactivity of the UN. The major Western powers on the Security Council would veto any effective sanctions against South Africa. Of course, Britain, France and the US have supported the racist South African regime because of their great economic interests in both Namibia and South Africa. For example, their multinational companies control the major mining industries in both Namibia and South Africa. To free Namibia, SWAPO could not sit back and wait to be liberated by outside forces. We decided that unless we started fighting, we would never be free. In 1962 our first cadres began military training in several friendly countries and we began preparing for armed struggle. In 1965 our first guerrilla units began underground activities inside Namibia, preparing to launch the armed struggle in 1966.

The South African regime has not officially banned SWAPO. Nevertheless, conditions inside Namibia are very difficult. Could you describe the political situation confronting SWAPO?

The fact is, though SWAPO is not officially banned by South Africa, our activities are under constant surveillance and harassment. The racist regime has proclaimed a State of Emergency in Namibia, known as Act 17, which sanctions harsh, police state measures, especially in the North, and denies SWAPO political rights. Effectively, SWAPO pamphlets are banned, our public meetings are threatened and sometimes prohibited, and our members are always in danger of arbitrary arrest. As a result, much of our organizing work must be done underground.

The Anti-Terrorism Act of 1967 (made retroactive to 1962) was aimed specifically against SWAPO freedom fighters. Under this act, many of our leaders were arrested and kept imprisoned in solitary confinement in Pretoria for more than a year without trial. In fact, SWAPO members are being arrested under this law every day. More than forty leaders and members are serving life-imprisonment on Robben Island .In other jails,our members are serving five to twenty-year sentences. Others still are under house arrest. Act 17 was used during the 1971–72 strikes when hundreds of workers were arrested. Recently, when the so-called multiracial constitutional talks started in Windhoek, thirty SWAPO members were locked up without trial in order to prevent demonstrations against the talks. However, not only are Namibians arrested by this racist regime, but our people have been tortured and cold-bloodedly murdered. We have even discovered mass graves with over 100 people buried inside. At Epinga in Openyama district, South African troops carried out a bloody massacre.

No, the Vorster regime has not pronounced SWAPO a banned organization, as it has done with the ANC or PAC of South Africa. But this is really just a diplomatic game because of pressure from the UN and the international community. This pressure has increased, especially since the position taken by the International Court of Justice in 1971, which clearly states that South Africa's occupation of Namibia is illegal.

There has been a long tradition of resistance in Namibia to colonial rule. Why has SWAPO achieved a higher stage of resistance after earlier struggles failed?

Well, the Germans colonized Namibia first, using the most brutal and racist methods. Our people strongly resisted German occupation. Especially the Hereros and the Namas in the central and southern regions fought heroically against the German invaders. But the Germans had superior armaments, and they nearly wiped out the population in these regions. Some writers estimate that the Herero tribe was reduced from 100,000 to 15,000. The Ovambos in the northern region also fought with the brothers to the South, as well as against the Portuguese colonialists, who were advancing from the North. There was long resistance to colonialism throughout Namibia, and it was carried on as late as 1932 by Chief Npumu of the Upunge. These earlier struggles failed because the people were fighting the foreign invaders in isolated struggles with inferior weapons. Now SWAPO has been able to mobilize the resistance against the South Africans at the national level. All tribal groupings in our nation are engaged in this struggle, despite the fact that the South African racist regime has tried by all means to maintain division by ethnic groupings.

Let's return to the war of national liberation that SWAPO is now waging and examine different aspects of it. How strong is SWAPO's popular support from the various parts of the population?

SWAPO is a mass movement, which means it is supported by the oppressed African majority. Workers, peasants, teachers, nurses and small businessmen are all involved in the national liberation struggle. The majority of Namibians are denied political rights and are suffering from hunger, disease and ignorance. Most are living in the rural "Bantustans" and this is where we draw most of our membership and fighters. PLAN (People's Liberation Army of Namibia) militants come from all sectors of the population—contract workers, women, youth. I might add that the youth of our country are the most militant in support of the movement. Of course, among the Africans there are some puppets, mostly chiefs, who agree to be used by the enemy, but in any nation you will find a few traitors.

Another sector of the population is the small community of "Coloreds." In an attempt to divide and rule, the South Africans have given them a special status which enables them to earn a little more money than Africans and gives them some other privileges. But they are not treated as Whites. As far as SWAPO is concerned, they are Namibians and they are Africans. There are also some puppets among the Coloreds who have been won over by self-interests, but a large part of the community does support SWAPO.

Then there are the minority white settlers, the ruling clique that enjoys the wealth of the country at the expense of the African majority. Unlike in South Africa, there have been no white progressive movements for African rights. Among the Whites here, very few have stood up and sided with the Africans in our just struggle. However, in SWAPO, we judge a person not by his color but by what he or she does. In an immediate sense, the fight today in Namibia is between the oppressed African masses and the oppressor white colonialists, because with few exceptions the Whites identify with colonialism.

In your operational areas, what are the relations between your militants and the civilian population who live and work the land?

Relations are very good. The guerrilla fighters have been able to operate there because the people support and protect them. They've been able to obtain food, clothing, and even money from the local population. Otherwise, it would be extremely difficult to survive. Sometimes the fighters are able to grow their own food. If not, they work alongside the local people in the fields. A guerrilla fighter cannot survive anywhere even for one hour without the support of the people. We have also created programs for medical care and basic education to serve the people in the rural areas, and this has helped earn our militants the people's confidence and support.

South Africa has responded to the liberation war by simultaneously stepping up their efforts for a neocolonial solution and increasing repression and terror directed at the civilian population. Part of this repression has been carried out by so-called tribal police who have been appointed by tribal chiefs, as in the so-called Owambo bantustan in Northern Namibia. What role do these chiefs and their police play and what is their relationship to the South African government?

One must make a distinction here when we talk about the chiefs. There are two kinds of chiefs. First there are the traditional chiefs who have supported the people's struggle for freedom. Because of this some of them were deposed by the South African government. For instance, Chief Ashikoto of the Odona tribe was removed because he would not cooperate with the enemy against his own people. And then you have the second type. These are puppets hand-picked by the South African government and put on the South African payroll. The enemy uses them as tools of oppression against the people. As far as SWAPO is concerned, they are traitors. This is the type of chief participating in the so-called multiracial constitutional talks. SWAPO is not against chiefs as such, but SWAPO is fighting against the South African government and this includes all of its collaborators.

You pointed out that the Namibian national liberation struggle unites a broad spectrum of the African population. What has been the role of the churches in this respect?

Many clergymen have clearly identified themselves with our struggle. Of course, at first colonialism used the churches to infiltrate African nations and pave the way for white settlement. But there's been a considerable change in the attitude of some churches—notably the Anglican Church, which has rejected the government policy and practice of racial discrimination and inferior education in its mission schools. As a result, most of its clergymen have been expelled from Namibia. Most of us in SWAPO are members of different religious groups in Namibia, while some priests actively participate in the liberation struggle as party members.

What role does the SWAPO organization inside Namibia and its organization outside the country have in directing the struggle? And what structures has SWAPO set up to organize this struggle from the base level up to the national executive?

First of all, the Congress of SWAPO adopts a program for build-ing the movement inside our country. Delegates from all sections of the party, particularly the leadership of these sections, participate in the Congress. Then the Central Committee acts as a policy-making body between sessions of the Congress. The National Executive Committee is elected by the Central Committee and has the duty to implement the program and all other party decisions made by the Congress.

Members of the Central Committee and National Executive are based both inside and outside Namibia. Subordinate to the National Executive are the regional headquarters, and then there are the smaller district branches or cells which sometimes have two or three hundred members. Departments have been established to provide for efficient running of specific areas of the organization. For ex-ample, there are the Departments of Education, Health, Defense and Transport, and Information and Publicity. We also have mass organizations representing different sectors of the people. For ex-ample, the workers are represented by the Labor Department and there is the Women's League and the Youth League. We also have the Council of Elders to mobilize the elderly people and to show them that we need them too, that every Namibian must be involved in the national liberation struggle, young and old.

How are decisions arrived at in SWAPO?

Our decisions are made through the democratic process of discus-sion and exchange of views at all levels. For instance, when the Cen-tral Committee meets, members from different regions come to ex-press their views. At the regional level, members express the views of the people of that particular region, and so on at each level.

Let's take a concrete example. How did SWAPO work out its posi-tion on the present constitutional talks in Windhoek?

Well, first our National Executive Committee met and concluded that SWAPO must oppose the constitutional talks. We completely rejected the ethnic grouping or "bantustan" concept. We demanded instead a democratic constitution under which the people could ex-press their views freely. Further, we maintained that any constitu-tional talks, or elections, should be supervised and controlled by the United Nations, not the South African government. We sent this position inside the country to our National Executive colleagues for their advice on whether there was any possible use in SWAPO's participating in these talks. Everyone at both the regional and district level was informed of this issue and fully discussed it. Our entire membership came to agree that these talks should be boycotted by SWAPO. As a result of such discussion throughout the organization, SWAPO arrived at a unified position on this important question.

What is the relation of PLAN to SWAPO?

The People's Liberation Army is the military wing of the party and not a separate organization. As such, it is recognized by the entire organization as the leading wing of the liberation struggle. The party as a whole is in fact moving step by step toward complete identification with the military wing. For instance, each member of the movement will be trained militarily in order to speed up the liberation of Namibia.

The Central Committee and the National Executive control the entire army. Cadres of PLAN are members of the Central Committee or National Executive. The Commander-in-Chief of PLAN is the President of the party and he is responsible for political leadership. Under the President is the Deputy Chief Commander who is commander of the army and responsible for all PLAN operations. Then there is the Secretary of Defense and Transport, who is in charge of all logistical operations, and reports to and advises the National Executive. Military operations are organized by the commanders of different regions who are responsible to make recommendations to the Secretary of Defense and Transport.

In a 1972 interview with LSM, your Director of Information briefly outlined the military situation then, saying that the People's Liberation Army of Namibia (PLAN) was carrying out operations in four regions—the Caprivi, Ovamboland, Kaokoveld and the Okavango. Combat action then consisted of planting of mines, small attacks and ambushes on South African patrols. Could you outline what has been happening at the military level since then?

During the past three years the People's Liberation Army has expanded military operations toward the central and southern regions, laying mines, setting ambushes and carrying out basic guerrilla warfare. Our progress is such that today we are in a position to destroy the enemy's military camps. Since the beginning of this year, our forces have completely wiped out four enemy camps. For proof of this, we have captured large quantities of armaments, radio communications and other equipment, including vehicles. Of course, the South African government would never acknowledge this. The South African Minister of Defense issued a statement that "terrorists" had attacked a military base which had been vacated by the South African troops. But you don't vacate a military camp and leave all your equipment behind! Our military advances are the reason that South Africa has sent more troops into Namibia. They are afraid that sooner or later, we will be in a position to stage a military campaign throughout the country.

Does your military strategy call for creating liberated areas in Namibia?

Certainly, our operational zones are expanding toward completely liberated areas. In some regions we have semi-liberated areas where the enemy can come with his ground troops only when they are supported by air cover. Still, the main objective of SWAPO is to liberate the entire country.

Are you considering urban tactics in the near future?

This is more difficult. In urban areas we encounter many difficulties because of our need for greater security. The racist police try to control these areas more closely and stage regular raids on the houses of the Africans. It is an extremely difficult situation. In the rural areas, however, we can mobilize the masses and they will give our fighters protection. Moreover, the enemy may pass by, but the guerrillas appear to be ordinary persons working and cultivating the land.

South Africa has tried to neutralize opposition with its bantustan policy. What does this mean to SWAPO?

As I mentioned, this racist regime will try any means to maintain division among the African people. Their slogan is: "Many nations within one country." Of course this is ridiculous. It is an accepted fact that countries often have more than one ethnic grouping. Switzerland, for example; more than three ethnic groupings compose that country. And yet there is only one Switzerland and citizens carry only one passport. SWAPO completely rejects South Africa's claim that the people of Namibia cannot be united in one nation because there are many ethnic groupings.

On the one hand, apartheid practices divide and rule among Africans; on the other hand, Whites are supposed to be one group irrespective of their different places of origin. In Namibia we have the Germans, the Boers and the English, as well as other nationals from different parts of Europe. All these, in South Africa's view, are one group, despite the fact that they speak different languages, have different cultures and come from different nations of Europe. And we, the Blacks, are supposed to be the Herero nation, the Ovambo nation, the Nama nation, the Kavango nation and what have you! SWAPO is resisting this Bantustan policy, for there is only one people, one nation in Namibia, irrespective of race or color or place of origin.

Another side of South African strategy is petty reform. Recently we've seen announcements that hotel owners have orders to take down their signs "Whites only," and there have been other moves against discrimination in public transportation and so on.

According to a *Windhoek Advertiser* report, Whites have been asked to scrap apartheid signs and allow Africans into hotels and restaurants—if they are well-dressed and the owners agree to accept Blacks. It is not a matter of policy that Blacks and Whites come and go freely wherever they live. Africans are still restricted by racist pass laws. But this "reform" is really for propaganda purposes outside Namibia. As far as SWAPO is concerned, we are not fighting merely to eliminate the apartheid racial discrimination. SWAPO is fighting to overthrow the illegal South African administration and to create a democratic state in Namibia.

Since the April coup in Portugal, the South African regime has done a lot of maneuvering—initiating contact with independent African countries, trying to bring about compromises with colonialism in Namibia and in Zimbabwe, as well as pursuing bantustan programs in South Africa. Inside Namibia, it has accelerated its bantustan schemes and sought some legitimacy by staging a "multi-racial" constitutional conference. How does SWAPO view these maneuvers?

Well South Arfica's "detente" policy should not mislead world opinion. If South Africa was really sincere and serious in this effort to create good relations with independent African states, surely it would start by withdrawing its troops from Namibia and allowing the United Nations to organize a democratic election based on the system of one-man, one-vote. But regardless of any peaceful appearances, South Africa is every day sending troops into Namibia, literally occupying every inch of Namibian soil. The regime holds phony elections and constitutional talks which are intended to divide our country on an ethnic basis and to cut off our support from the international community. While South Africa talks of peaceful solutions, it is actually training African puppet troops to fight against SWAPO freedom fighters. South Africa has allocated millions of dollars to its state security forces (BOSS) for bribes, propaganda against SWAPO. It has even employed former police agents and soldiers from the Portuguese colonial army in Angola. It must be clearly understood that a peaceful solution to the Namibian problem is a remote prospect. We have no other alternative but to intensify the armed liberation struggle as the only effective way to achieve freedom and independence.

Conscripting Africans to fight Africans seems to have become a basic tool of counterinsurgency in the area. Haven't the South Africans also created strategic hamlets in an effort to isolate your militants from the population?

Yes, especially in the eastern Caprivi Strip, the Okavango, and in some parts of the northern region, they have forcibly moved the people from their traditional lands into strategic hamlets. Here they plant their informers and often surround the hamlets with military camps. This is what is happening in the district of Okolongo. They are trying to deny us contact with the masses and cut off our guerrilla fighters' food supply. But we still manage to destroy the enemy. Our attacks are always carefully planned after good reconnaissance. When attacking enemy camps, we employ tactics and weapons (mostly small arms) which avoid as much as possible any fire on the captive African population. The South Africans' aim is to create the impression that SWAPO guerrillas are "bandits" who are killing all the people, Blacks as well as Whites. But the people know the guerrillas and have confidence in them. We certainly also try to avoid killing innocent Whites. Primarily we attack military installations and soldiers.

Are there any conditions under which SWAPO would enter into negotiations with South Africa?

Let me make SWAPO's position very clear. The only conditions for any peaceful solution to the Namibian problem are: first, South Africa must publicly state that the people of Namibia have the right to self-determination and national sovereignty; secondly, South Africa must recognize the territorial integrity of Namibia; thirdly, South Africa must renounce its evil Bantustan policy in Namibia; fourthly, South Africa must release all political prisoners and allow exiles to return to Namibia; and finally, South Africa must withdraw its troops and security forces from Namibia. These are the conditions on which SWAPO will participate in negotiations to end the illegal South African colonial administration.

What are your major sources of support, including political, finan-

cial and military, outside the country?

Most of our support comes from the Organization of African Unity (OAU) and from the socialist countries, as well as organizations and individuals in the Western World. We receive moral and political support from the United Nations and its special agencies and in some cases material assistance. UNESCO, for example, has provided us with educational facilities and equipment. Third World countries have given us considerable moral encouragement and, in addition, generous material assistance. Tanzania and Zambia especially have played a great role in providing us with material support and in allowing our people to live in their countries.

What do you think international pressure—for example, expelling South Africa from the UN—can do to advance your struggle?

We always appreciate political and material support. So far, world public opinion has been able to mobilize sentiment especially in the United Nations and other international organizations against South Africa and in support of our national liberation struggle. But support from the international community by itself would not be sufficient to bring about the liquidation of South African colonialism in Namibia. The Namibians themselves must be totally involved in the fight, ready and able to wage a protracted armed struggle.

Much of the Namibian economy is owned or controlled by large multinational corporations which have their base in North America and Europe, as well as in South Africa itself. What kind of pressure do you think can and should be brought to bear on these corporations?

One important way to bring pressure on both South Africa and the multinationals exploiting the wealth of Namibia is to mobilize local trade unions to boycott shipping lines which are handling goods manufactured and extracted from Namibia. Too often resolutions are passed in the UN General Assembly and then just filed away and forgotten. For this reason, SWAPO has attempted to bring up the matter of Namibia directly with the masses of people of individual members states. It is important that trade unions, students and even MPs or Congressmen be mobilized to raise the question of Namibia with their governments. Various resolutions of the UN demand that the member states sever diplomatic, economic and trade relations with South Africa. So it is very important to mobilize forces to pressure these individual countries to meet their responsibilities.

Realistically, how much support do you expect from a government like the Canadian government, which on the one hand supports UN anti-apartheid resolutions but on the other allows Canadian companies like Falconbridge to continue extracting raw materials—and superprofits—from Namibia?

This is not a difficult question for me to answer. Many western countries have been very hypocritical. While paying lip-service to UN resolutions, those countries maintaining diplomatic and economic relations with South Africa continue supporting this apartheid regime. Britain, France and the US prevent South Africa from being expelled from the UN, and others join in keeping economic sanctions and arms embargos from being imposed. We consider to be our enemy those who support racist South Africa in any way—politically, militarily or economically. Therefore, we look for support among the masses in these countries—anti-imperialist organizations, trade unions and student groups. This is our real source of support.

What lessons have you drawn from the past decade of African independence in relation to your own efforts for the future of Namibia?

We have been watching the economic development of African countries and the rest of the Third World. And I think we've gained many insights into how we can attack our own economic problems in order to raise the standard of living of our people, who for centuries have been oppressed by colonialism. Once our people are free from colonial oppression they will be looking forward with enthusiasm to building their nation. SWAPO is already preparing to lead the development of a free Namibia. For instance, at the Namibia Health and Education Center in Zambia, we are developing our cadre, education and health programs. While we conduct literacy and other classes for the increasing numbers of exiled Namibians escaping from the South African repression, we are also training cadres in agriculture, motor mechanics and other fields. Our PLAN units have also gained important experience in carrying out our medical and other programs inside the country. Our objective is to train ourselves in all fields and achieve political self-reliance. With independence, we will be prepared to expand from this base to meet the immediate needs of our people and develop our country. Developing agriculture will be our main priority. Namibia is an underdeveloped country with the majority of the population engaged in subsistence agriculture. It is important to develop our agricultural base so that we won't have to import food from other countries and can save our resources to import only essential material, such as machinery, medical supplies, etc.

To pursue this a little further, what would you say are likely to be some of the policies of a SWAPO government in politically independent Namibia?

Well, with regard to foreign policy, a SWAPO government will adopt a posture of neutrality and non-alignment. SWAPO, of course, will have diplomatic relations with all countries in the world which are friendly toward our country. We are Pan-Africanists, so we'll play a very active part in the OAU and will promote the objectives of closer economic cooperation and continental political unity. We will also become members of the United Nations, in order to contribute in our own small way, as a small country, to the progress of mankind in general. Within Namibia we'll have a policy of equal distribution of the wealth of our country for the benefit of all our people. For instance, the SWAPO government will see to it that there will be free education from primary to university level. Now this means that profits from our copper, uranium, diamonds, etc., must be used to support free education, free medical treatment, and other services which will be provided free to the people.

But to be able to tap the surplus from the extraction of Namibia's natural wealth, you will probably have to take full control over the existing operations of the corporations. Are you talking about nationalizing key industries, or all industries?

Certainly our government will control all the national wealth. Some of the multinational corporations may be allowed to continue their operations under new agreements. But the exploitation of Namibian workers and uncontrolled extraction of Namibian wealth would not be allowed to continue. We will ensure that Blacks and Whites will receive fair and equal wages for the same work. It's clearly stated in many resolutions of the United Nations that foreign companies operating in Namibia under the South African administration are doing so illegally. Under a SWAPO government no such exploitation will be allowed to continue!

Presently, the most productive land in the country is in the hands of a relatively small group of wealthy White farmers. How will you deal with the question of land?

According to South African laws, no African in Namibia is allowed to own land. The South African government has the right to remove Africans from one place to another anywhere throughout the country. This policy would be immediately abolished and the land monopolized by the minority white settlers would be made available to everybody in the country. We cannot allow a continuation of minority settler ownership and exploitation, while the majority of Africans have no land to live on. After all, this is what we are fighting for. Are we not fighting to liberate Namibia for all Namibians to enjoy a better life?

With a SWAPO government in power, do you expect that a lot of Whites will leave the country?

A large number of Whites may leave, because many Whites in Namibia are fascist, particularly among the Germans, who are the second largest white group in Namibia. I suspect that most will not accept African rule. Many have already sold their property and are staying in hotels so that they can leave quickly of SWAPO should come to power. Many will probably go to Germany or to South Africa. Many Afrikaaners too are extremely racist and will not accept African rule. Many of them are South Africans and were brought here by the government, so they will probably pick up and go back to South Africa before our independence. But this will be entirely up to them. If they accept majority rule, they are welcome to stay.

The various ideological struggles over differences within the socialist camp present a number of problems for liberation movements, as well as independent political organizations such as LSM. How has SWAPO dealt with this situation?

You might expect some difficulty since this ideological conflict involves big powers who offer us considerable material support. But we accept only genuine support with no strings attached. Countries that are supporting us must accept the fact that they are supporting a genuine struggle for national liberation. If they give us support expecting SWAPO to side with them in conflicts with other countries, then we will refuse their aid.

After independence what kind of relations do you anticipate with those powers, such as the US, Germany, Canada and Japan, which today support the South African regime and whose multinational corporations play a direct role in exploiting Namibia's people and resources?

This will depend on the attitude of these countries toward an independent Namibia. If their attitude is negative, well, we have been fighting a long time and we will continue to resist any kind of threat from any quarter in the world. If those powers or countries adopt a friendly attitude toward us, we'll have a good relationship with them, provided of course that we put an end to their multinationals' exploitation of our wealth.

But historical experience, in Chile for example, and other countries, certainly indicates that these powers will go very far in order to retain their stranglehold on Namibia and to retain their positions of wealth and power. To what extent are you prepared to deal with efforts like this on the part of imperialist powers?

SWAPO is an anti-imperialist organization and we will not permit the continuation of imperialist exploitation of our mineral wealth or the oppression of our people. We are fighting against it now, and will continue to fight against it when Namibia is free!

In the process of your struggle you have forged certain links with progressive forces in the capitalist countries who support your struggle. Do you expect to continue these relations after independence and if so, concretely, how do you think they can continue?

I think we will continue to improve established relationships with progressive forces in the capitalist world. We are promoting certain common objectives; we are fighting for improvement of the conditions of all people. In other words, the forces of SWAPO and the progressive forces in the capitalist nations are part and parcel of the internationalist struggle for progress of all mankind—for the end of exploitation of man by man.

So when it's our turn to wage an armed struggle, then we can turn to a free Namibia to support us?

I will welcome that!

An
Army
To
Serve
The
Exploited
Masses

Military and political instruction
at SWAPO camp
inside Namibia - MPLA photo

Comrade Kakauru Nganjone has been a member of SWAPO since 1960, when he was seventeen. In 1970, after study and military training abroad, Nganjone joined the People's Liberation Army of Namibia (PLAN). As a PLAN militant he took part in many operations and worked in a number of capacities. In 1972 Comrade Nganjone was appointed by the Party to the post of Political Commissar of PLAN, a responsibility he continues to carry out today.

Kakauru Nganjone was interviewd by LSM's Ole Gjerstad in Lusaka, Zambia, in October, 1975.

To begin with, Comrade Nganjone, what is the relationship between PLAN and the non-military organs of SWAPO, and what is your role in this?

President Sam Nujoma, the leader of our Party, is also the Commander-in-Chief of the Army. Directly under him sits the National Executive, which is made up of various departments, e.g. Department of Information, Department of Defense, and so on. As the Political Commissar of PLAN, I work with the Department of Defense and serve as a link between the National Executive and the military. This means that I am responsible for communicating and clarifying party policy, party decisions and military strategy with PLAN commanders and with other political commissars under my leadership. I am also responsible for the overall political development and morale of all SWAPO militants.

Perhaps you could discuss how people are recruited into the armed struggle—and some of the concerns and problems SWAPO encounters among the people.

First of all, comrade, you know the situation in Namibia: we have been denied all human rights. Our people are tired of being under the repressive rule of South Africa. Most Namibians are workers. If they're not workers, then they're semi-workers or peasants. But a new generations of peasants does not exist in our country; only the old people who are left at home to till the land. The others have been forced to go away to find jobs in the Police Zone. They go to the factories in Walvis Bay, in Tsumeb, in Windhoek . . . or they go to work on the farms, as domestics or gardeners. They work for the Boers on Boer terms; on contracts like slaves, for very little money, with miserable treatment and frequent beatings and arrests. They are tired of this; they are enraged and willing to take on the Boers any way they can. We in SWAPO talk to the people, telling them that we cannot accept these conditions—and that we don't have to. We want our country back, to work our own land in freedom.

So in our recruitment, we first talk to people about their lives and the oppression they have experienced. And we find that everyone wants to add his own experiences to what we are talking about. Then we explain who are the people's friends, who are our enemies, and how we can best fight them. In the course of our discussions, we explain the nature of apartheid and talk about Namibia's history, and in this way help create a wider world outlook. It is not difficult to convince the people of the need to fight South African oppression. It is more difficult to convince them of the proper methods of fighting.

When people first join SWAPO, some of them just want to kick the enemy out of Namibia. But when you ask him, "How are you going to fight him?" he says, "Any way I can! I'll strike, sabotage my work machine . . . I'll fight with stones, bottles, anything!" Others believe that the powers of the United Nations or other friendly organizations will win Namibia back for them. But that is not how we view it. We think that the only way to defeat South Africa is through organized armed struggle.

So as a political commissar, you give this desire for change a political orientation and turn it into a powerful tool for the liberation of Namibia. Concretely, how do you educate your militants?

In our camps, we carry out both military training and political education. We hold regular discussions covering such things as Namibia's colonization, our people's resistance, and SWAPO's history and political program. Since we haven't many books, which are expensive and hard for us to come by, most learning takes place through discussion.

When we discuss our history, we talk about how South Africa took over from the Germans and began setting up the contract labor system; how African land was taken over to satisfy the demands of the increasing white settler population, while our people were moved off to reserves, lands unfit for human habitation. We talk about SWANLA—the white-controlled agency designed to supply labor for white farms and mines. We talk about how foreign corporations have taken over our natural resources and how the whole apartheid system was supposedly legalized in 1948. We talk about how the people resisted those changes and study the numerous uprisings and rebellions that preceded our revolution. Then we explain how we sought freedom through the United Nations, the OAU, and other international organizations, and how—despite repeated resolutions and promises—our people are still under the same South African rule. Why? Because many nations in the United Nations are imperialist and benefit from South African apartheid. We are fighting not only South Africa; South Africa itself is a satellite of the big imperialist powers. So, we teach our militants that our main enemy is imperialism, represented by South Africa. We also identify our second enemy: those who work for or support the racist regime against the interests of the masses . . . the opportunists and puppets on the payroll of the South African Government, making a living off our people today. We talk about how to deal with these elements from our past experience in our home towns and work areas.

Mainly, though, we discuss the importance of fighting the enemy through armed struggle. In this struggle, our cadres must be educated about SWAPO and our program of action; they must know why they are fighting. What are we after? What do we want today? And tomorrow? What do we want after we achieve our freedom and independence?

We are waging a war, a liberation war which must be fought arms-in-hand by the Namibian people themselves. Therefore, our first task is to build a party capable of mobilizing the masses. We must organize our struggle through a strong, united force—with one voice, one party, and one leadership. The demands on us are extraordinary. We must be extraordinary ourselves. To wage a revolutionary struggle, we must be a vanguard party, leading the workers and peasants. We must be well organized at every level; in our leadership, in our camps, in our guerrilla units. By building the People's Liberation Army, we are also building a core of political cadres who will act as catalysts within the country during the armed struggle and after independence. These cadres will be the ones to educate the people about the way we want Namibia to be. They will fight for the well-being of our people and educate the young ones toward a revolutionary spirit.

We are people who are fighting for a just cause, shedding blood for our freedom. We want a free and democratic Namibia. We will build a true democracy that will serve the poor and exploited masses. After independence the Namibian people will choose; the wind of freedom will give them the direction. These very guerrilla fighters are going to see to it that our people are not suppressed or exploited again, that nothing is taken away from the people. That is what we are fighting for, the well-being of our people. . . . These things are an essential part of our political education.

We also educate people about tribalism and nationalism. We explain that our party program is based on equality among our people;

that a person of any race, color or sex is accepted warmly into our ranks. We have to stress the unity of the Namibian people and counter the divide-and-rule tactics employed by the South African fascists, who set people of different tribes against each other. We try to educate our people in common understanding, in cooperation. Before, when the white man first colonized our country, people were resisting separately, but today we have a vanguard party and are more mature politically. Now people from all tribes must befriend each other, must learn the culture and language of one another, must understand each other—so that we can go ahead together as a united people. This is a very important question in doing mass political work.

Do you discuss other liberation struggles?

Yes, we try to learn from the experience of other revolutionary movements. Africa is a new continent; all the independent countries got their freedom within the last ten to fifteen years. We cite the revolutions of those who fought with guns in their hands. First of all, the peoples of Algeria and Kenya: we study their struggles and try to learn from both their successes and failures. Also the people of Guinea, the people of the Congo during the time of Lumumba, then the people in the Arab Republic of Egypt who also brought down the colonial yoke. Then too, the heroic people of Viet Nam, Laos and Cambodia; we discuss the Korean war, the Chinese revolution, and the October Revolution in the Soviet Union, where the first socialist country was established. We talk about Cuba and Latin America, where movements are also building a strong socialism and anti-imperialism, just like on the African continent. We study these examples, and discuss why one revolution triumphed, while others failed. We even discuss developments in capitalist countries, like the Paris Commune. We try to find out why did this happen, how could this or that situation have been better handled, and when similar problems reveal themselves in Namibia, how we can best handle them.

We try to create an understanding of all progressive forces fighting to end capitalism and imperialism in this world. We are a national liberation movement, and we want to end imperialism in Namibia first of all. But the workers and peasants of our country are also part and parcel of the world revolutionary process. Therefore we try to give them an understanding of the importance of proletarian internationalism.

What are the conditions in which this training is carried out? What

is the camp routine in terms of the militants' daily schedules, duties and tasks outside of straight combat situations?

In our training camps we have a regular weekly schedule. We get up by six o' clock every morning. We go through our morning exercises, stop for tea and something to eat, then we go to our daily training, classes or duties. At around noon we break for lunch, take one to two hours of rest, then resume training or study activities. After the evening meal, some comrades continue their duties while others might just relax together—depending on what duties a person has for that day. On the weekends, we do washing and other tasks and sometimes cultural things or sports like football. As in all guerrilla wars, however, the conditions are very tough. Our guerrillas must often sleep outside with all their belongings; sometimes we have to go for long periods without food or sleep. Now in our camps we must prepare the comrades for these conditions. All of us must get used to them. So sacrifices are a necessary part of training in our camps. Learning to make sacrifices steels our militants so that they can be strong in fighting the enemy and can stand up under all circumstances.

How do they respond to these difficult training conditions? What kinds of problems do you have to deal with?

Well, comrade, in the beginning it's very difficult, as some of our new recruits aren't used to such discipline and hardship. For example, some don't like to get up so early, and they say, "Ah, I am sick,"—wanting to sleep a little longer. Here the political commissars like myself step in. We say, "Do you think you are benefiting yourself? No, your indiscipline benefits the enemy! We can't win our struggle with soldiers like you! Look at Comrade so-and-so. He is always punctual and disciplined. He can be relied upon to carry out responsibilities!" When that person is criticized and comes to understand better, he begins to struggle daily to improve his behavior. After two to three months, it seems normal to be up and working at six o'clock.

Do you have cases where, after experiencing hardships, some people want to give up and go home? If so, how do you deal with it?

This is a rare phenomenon. All of our guerrillas are volunteers; they come to us with a strong motivation to fight. But before a comrade joins PLAN we discuss the difficulties involved, so that he or she knows that sacrifices are part of the struggle for liberation. When his morale gets low, we struggle with that comrade to strengthen his political understanding and keep him within our ranks. Under certain circumstances, however, when a unit camp is near the person's home and we feel it would be safe both personally and politically for him to go, we sometimes allow him to return home for a while.

What is SWAPO's view towards integrating women into the armed struggle, how do you do so, and what problems do you confront?

In our struggle every militant, whether male or female, plays an equal role. We want everyone to contribute fully according to his or her capacity. Old patterns, however, can restrict our freedom to act in new ways. Therefore we have certain guidelines and rules. For example, single men and women have separate quarters in the training camps. If a couple wants to live together, then they must become married. If husband and wife are in the same training camp, they may share their quarters. We cannot afford loose relationships between men and women; we must develop mutual respect among comrades. We are in this struggle to defeat a powerful enemy, and to defeat this enemy we must use all our human resources.

Do you have problems combatting traditional male attitudes towards women, that women are weaker and less capable?

I think this attitude is a disease all over the world, and one that we are not immune from. In the past there was a view that the women are always weak, that they should bring up children, take care of the home, prepare food and so on, but not play a leading role in the struggle or fight militarily. Now, we strongly discourage the men from looking down on female fighters, as this is destructive to our common goals. And the women must also overcome feelings of inferiority and not be afraid to take on large responsibilities. But there are some problems. For example, we now have two female commanders. In the beginning some men were trying to disobey or get around their orders. In these cases, we had stern discussions with the militants involved and told them that these women were given such responsibilities and powers by the Party because of their intelligence and capacity. Through open criticism and self-criticism, we are able to deal with these problems on an ongoing basis.

How would you describe relations between PLAN militants and their leaders?

Leaders must set a good example in their comportment, lifestyle, and political judgement. Most of all, they must win the confidence of those working under them. The guerrillas must have a firm confidence in their commander during battle. This type of leadership, of course, is developed over time and through the process of criticism and struggle. Once a leader makes a decision around a particular course of action, the rank and file have the strict responsibility to follow this course wholeheartedly. If a militant is unsure of a decision being right or not, he or she must bring it up at the appropriate time. Sometimes this is before an action, sometimes after. Obviously, we can't have criticisms coming up in the middle of a battle. We have regular opportunities for review and criticism at all levels of SWAPO and PLAN. In these reviews the leadership must be ready and willing to learn everything possible from the mistakes made. They must listen closely to all criticism and take concrete steps to improve their behavior.

How do you prepare the militants politically for combat?

Political commissars work hand-in-hand with the commanders of military units. I help out with planning an attack or an operation, how we should organize ourselves, what the political considerations are, etc. I help with morale by explaining to the militants the difficulties we may confront; for example, whether we'll have sufficient cover, what the size and equipment of our enemy will be, whether we'll be able to pick up enemy weapons afterwards, how long we may have to wait in ambush, etc. Then, whenever possible, I participate in the action with the fighters.

What are the key factors you take into account in keeping up the morale of the militants?

Firstly, we must know the enemy. Secondly, we must know ourselves and how well we are prepared for certain operations. Thirdly, we must know the terrain and the people in any given area of operation. With these factors in mind, we can plan successful strategy and keep morale up.

In 1972 your Director of Information indicated to us that SWAPO was carrying out military operations in four zones. What developments have taken place since then?

Developments in this field have been really tremendous, especially in Okavango and the Caprivi Strip. The South African Government made attempts to seal the borders of those regions to destroy SWAPO bases. They killed many people suspected of SWAPO affiliation and arrested many more. This terrorism, however, further

46

strengthened our relations with the people, and support for SWAPO has grown even stronger. Our fighters have now penetrated very deeply into the country and we are operating in six regions. Those deep inside do mostly organizational work, preparing the people for the day when we will see a total revolt throughout the country. In the urban areas we are preparing to carry out urban guerrilla warfare, as many of our people there are more politically conscious.

In the beginning years of our struggle, most of our actions were on a small scale, such as planting mines and ambushing enemy troops. Recently we launched large-scale attacks with much heavier armaments than were available in the past. These we captured from South African camps. We are in the process of transforming some of our military units from guerrilla units to semi-guerrilla regular army units so that we can carry out decisive large-scale attacks where South Africa is vulnerable. To carry out these attacks, we are organized into sections, platoons and detachments. A section is composed of about fifteen militants; a platoon of three sections; and a detachment of three platoons (or about a hundred and thirty-five fighters). For a large attack, we may employ up to one detachment.

Where is the South African Government strongest, and what tactics do they employ against SWAPO?

The South African Army is concentrated in the northern half of the country where they have a number of big military bases: at Grootfontein, Runtu, Katima Mulilo, also Gobabis in the East. As the armed struggle has intensified, their troops and weaponry have become more sophisticated. In the beginning they used many helicopters. Now they are using heavier weapons like fighter-bombers, small planes, tanks and armored cars. They are also utilizing mercenaries from PIDE and the Portuguese Army. With Angolan independence, they joined the South African Army and, after ideological training in Tsumeb, have been stationed largely in Grootfontein. Many of these have participated in the invasion of Angola, since they'd been near the Cunene Dam, and were so familiar with the border area.

The Boers also use strategic hamlets in the North, trying to isolate the guerrillas from the people. The people are enclosed by these hamlets and must pass by guards to go in or out. The guards—"home guards" or tribal police—also patrol adjoining areas and villages, and try to keep an eye on all movements. This way they hope to discourage contact between the guerrillas and the people. But their tactics have not been too successful. Our guerrillas are still able to keep in touch with the people, and many in the hamlets are rising up. Such tactics only reveal the insecurity of the South African forces and their mounting fear of our strong relations with the masses.

Poisoning the water is another tactic. The South Africans have poisoned many rivers and ponds. This has killed civilians and destroyed crops, especially in the Okavango and Caprivi Strip. This was accompanied by indiscriminate killing; dropping herbicides on crops; burning gardens, homes and fields. These tactics have presented problems, but we are overcoming them. For example, we know the country well and have water sources they don't know about.

The South Africans also have brutal methods of dealing with captured prisoners. They torture them severely to make them talk about our plans and the location of our camps; most of our people would rather die silently than help this enemy. But really the South Africans are very much afraid. Sometimes they get jumpy and shoot at anything that moves . . . we even heard this story about South African troops capturing a crocodile—or maybe it was a lizard—and taking it in to give it high voltage electric shocks. Maybe South African soldiers really believe that guerrillas can turn themselves into animals, but at least we know that SWAPO militants have a reputation for being elusive and tough. One captured soldier said, "We can be walking around, fighting no one, and suddenly find we are under fire or bombed. We never know what to expect!" So, you see, they are very frightened, and take this out on their prisoners.

What is SWAPO's policy on captured prisoners?

We treat our prisoners well. We move them to a safe place and talk to them. We educate them, to let them know that we are people too. We talk about our struggle for freedom, why we are fighting, and what role they as South African soldiers play. In our talks many of them say they were forced to fight by the South African government and never wanted to go to the bush. They say that they are tired of their terrible lives of walking in the hot sun for days and days and seeing nobody, then suddenly getting shot at. Many of the African soldiers were conscripted. They were first arrested, then perhaps told to go to work as a guard somewhere, only to find themselves in the army training to fight the guerrillas. They say they've seen several of their troops who refused to fight shot on the spot. They don't want to fight. Many of them surrender without any wounds. After talking to them, and also trying to gather any useful information, we hand them over to our headquarters, and then they are sent to the Red Cross or into political asylum.

How does SWAPO deal with logistics, medical care and subsistence for the guerrillas?

We have very few medical facilities for treating the guerrillas and the people. We do have some paramedics and nurses, but their knowledge is fairly limited. We have no experienced doctors who can remove bullets or perform surgery.

We have also had some difficulties with logistics, especially in our move from guerrilla to semi-guerrilla army units. Our weaponry is heavier and more difficult to transport. We do, however, use horses and sometimes even cars or captured tanks to transport our militants, weapons, and wounded.

Our guerrillas try to be self-sufficient in terms of food. At this point we have set up some fields where PLAN grows food for itself. We also capture food from the enemy, and are given food by the people. Where we can't have SWAPO fields, we try to work with the people on their fields and they share their food with us. This works out quite well, because our relations with the people are good. They always try to work with us and help us, even though they are under very heavy repression and could be killed. When we go into a region where there has been no previous PLAN or SWAPO activity we first engage in political education. We tell the people what our objectives and programs are. We are very careful about how we act, to counteract the Boer's propaganda that we are bandits and thieves. We help them in their work, and sometimes teach them other things. Working with them, we win their confidence, and they are willing to help us with food or whatever they can to help free Namibia.

Perhaps you could comment on your relation to Angola. Many Angolans used to go on contract to Namibia, and Namibians worked in Angola. The Kwanyama people live on both sides of the border. What has this proximity and interaction meant for your struggle?

The peoples of Africa are bound by a certain unity, and in this case the Kwanyama people only give Angola and Namibia a stronger basis for a close relationship. We are not going to fight over our borders. We believe that an African is an African . . . maybe tomorrow we will be heading toward a "United States of Africa." The partition of Africa was made by the imperialist powers without the African peoples' consent, but this is now becoming a matter for our own consideration. We are all struggling for African unity; some day perhaps we will remove all borders between countries, because we are the same people. We will fight hand-in-hand with our Angolan compatriots of the MPLA whenever necessary. We will continue to support them in their struggle.

Our organization is working to supply SWAPO with a printshop which will serve to further develop educational aspects of SWAPO's work through publication of revolutionary textbooks and propaganda, and will also help SWAPO make its struggle known to progressive people around the world. What is your attitude toward internationalist projects like this one?

Internationalism is a very important factor in our struggle. We have close comradely relations with many countries and organizations throughout the world. These people help us advance our struggle for liberation. Your organization also plays a part. As I said before, we have a great shortage of books with which to teach our militants and the people. Education is an essential part of liberation. Having a printshop will certainly help in overcoming the illiteracy and ignorance imposed on our people. With the help of our friends, we will win our struggle for liberation. We have the support of many people throughout the world, who are genuinely helping us with no strings attached. This is important.

Day
Of
The
Cobra

Defenders of
white supremacy

As a soldier of the South African army, Bill Anderson was witness to many of the inhuman methods employed by South Africa in its "Operation Cobra," the massive security sweep of Namibia's northern border area. Here is part of his story:

My name is Bill Anderson. I was born in Cape Town in 1955 and I was called up into the 6th Battalion, South African Infantry (SAI), on July 2, 1975. I did my basic training at Grahamstown. My number was 7153773 BA and I served on operations in a HQ Platoon. . . .

Our battalion covered about 200 square kilometers up to the border. We had helicopter support, based with a paratroop battalion at Ondongwa. This was all known as Operation Cobra. Our patrols, which were on foot, usually lasted about three days. Torture began almost at once when the suspects were brought back. The first few were interrogated by a section of 10 South African police inside the tent of battalion HQ. I saw the troops beating the suspects with rifles and fists and kicks for two hours before they were taken into the tent. All the troops were welcome to join in the beating.

Whenever torture was going on, either in battalion HQ or in the open space behind, a crowd would gather to watch. I would not watch but every night I heard the screams. Torture would begin at about 9 pm. The screams would go on until well after midnight. Officers boasted in front of me of using field telephones for electric shock torture to the genitals, nipples, and ears. It was common knowledge that this was being done.

I saw two suspects given water torture at the camp near Inahna. Their heads were stuffed into an ordinary iron bucket full of water and they were held under until they ceased to struggle. It lasted a good minute. I saw one large suspect who struggled so that five men had to hold him into the bucket.

I often saw young boys being roughly manhandled and kicked. They were blindfolded. Some were about 13 and some a little older.

All suspects were blindfolded and beaten when brought in. The conditions they were kept in were appalling. They were handcuffed to trees at night. Some were kept in pits. It was winter and very cold, approaching freezing point at night. Suspects were handcuffed to trees, dressed only in loincloths and drenched in cold water.

I was the cook and the only food I know they were given was scraps once a day which were piled in a big bin. On the average, they were interrogated by our battalion for two days before being 'coptered back to Ondongwa.

Early in June the five battalions mounted a joint operation, sweeping in to the center. My battalion swept down from near the border, while other battalions moved in from the flanks toward a stop battalion in the South. My battalion swept 100 sq. km., with one section per kilometer, moving one km. a day. Every male over the age of puberty was brought in. The orders were to kill those who ran and arrest those who did not run. All the arrested men were beaten, tortured, and interrogated without exception. They were then taken to Ondongwa.

Our battalion captured between 200 and 300 men, and the other battalions captured a similar number, I believe. Of the 1,000 or so detained men, we were later told that 40 were to be charged with ter- ism offences. All went to Ondongwa where those not charged were ordered to fill sandbags endlessly while soldiers emptied them and ordered the men to fill them again. They filled the bags with their bare hands.

Reprinted from the *Guardian* (London), September 5, 1976.

53

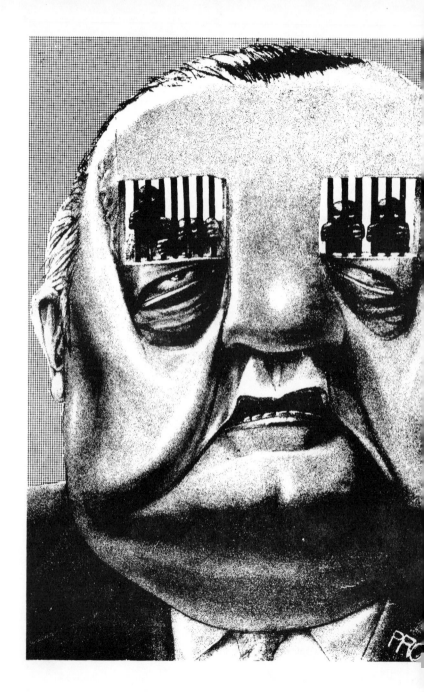

The South African Propaganda Offensive

- Amandla graphic

The following article was released by SWAPO's Department of Information and Publicity in December 1977.

Faced with intensified political and military resistance by SWAPO, as well as with diplomatic pressure by the international community, the South African government has been forced to concede, at least in theory, that there can be no internationally or internally acceptable solution in Namibia which excludes SWAPO. While it talks of negotiations and a "peaceful solution," however, it is continuing to consolidate its armed occupation of the country. South Africa's complete refusal to withdraw its 50,000 troops from Namibia, indicates its commitment to preventing a SWAPO victory in Namibia, even through the ballot box.

Now the latest South African offensive in Namibia is a massive propaganda campaign against SWAPO. This takes many forms, but is centered on three basic lines of attack: the promotion of racism and tribalism, a newfound and totally unconvincing South African attachment to the democratic process, and the age-old communist scare. The tactics used are those of force and intimidation, with South African soldiers both spreading anti-SWAPO propaganda and perpetrating atrocities for which they blame SWAPO "terrorists." Anonymous leaflets and propaganda tracts regularly flood the black locations, farms, and reserves. Anti-SWAPO comic books, written in several Namibian languages, have covers depicting an armed African gunning down a white priest. Leaflets show SWAPO President Sam Nujoma and Daniel Tjongarero (SWAPO Vice-Chairman) with lions' heads, devouring little children. SWAPO publicity materials are, on the other hand, banned if they are not produced inside Namibia.

The latest series of South African pamphlets is geared towards the proposed elections in 1978 and concentrates on the accusation that SWAPO fears an election because it does not have the support of the people of Namibia. The "violence" of SWAPO is contrasted with the "peace" of the Turnhalle.

"SWAPO is Communist." "Support the Turnhalle and not the country of Communism" read the posters, long after the Turnhalle constitutional conference (aimed at dividing Namibia into 11 bantustans) is supposed to have been dissolved. SWAPO is being depicted as murderous, terroristic, bloodthirsty, undemocratic, currupt, directionless, leaderless, and at the mercy of its communist masters in Russia and Cuba. One leaflet shows SWAPO President Sam Nujoma grovelling at Castro's feet; Castro is armed with Soviet weapons. "Who is going to pay for all the Soviet arms and how will it be paid for? It is us who will have to pay for it with our own blood." "Terror and death is the only way of the leaders of SWAPO and their Communist comrades."

South Africa's attempt to use the image of the Red Menace to cajole the Namibian people into supporting its Turnhalle puppets and opposing SWAPO has however backfired. In the words of one Namibian, "South Africa tells us that SWAPO is communist. But we know that SWAPO is fighting for the liberation of the Namibian people. If that is communism, then we are all for it."

Following the publication of a series of SWAPO leaflets, entitled "Turnhalle puppets," the South Africans reacted by calling SWAPO the "South West Africa Puppets Organization" and are now producing their own "puppet" leaflets with Samora Machel, Agostinho Neto, and Sam Nujoma dancing on strings pulled by Castro. In September they even produced a fake issue of "Ombuze ya Namibia," the monthly SWAPO bulletin produced and distributed in Namibia. This false issue included an editorial supposed to be from President Nujoma, admitting that SWAPO was killing innocent people in northern Namibia and saying that SWAPO soldiers were trained to kill. In fact, so much time was spent on that important matter that very little time was left for anything else! And in an attempt to extort money from the Namibian people, it asked them to send urgently needed financial assistance to SWAPO foreign missions with addresses in Havana and London.

For the South African government propaganda is big business. They have the use of South African and local puppet radio stations, the press, police, armed forces, spies, and above all, money. They have funded the "Pro-SWA Foundation," whose director is a former SWAPO member now turned renegade and self-styled Professor, Mburumba Kerina. Pro-SWA's job is to promote the Turnhalle, although like the Turnhalle itself, its existence and activity is basically anti-SWAPO. On its formation Pro-SWA launched an appeal for a preliminary $1,200,000 and approached major western companies operating in Namibia, including Rio Tinto Zinc and the US-owned Tsumeb corporation. Funds were also sought from West Germany, and many German businessmen and residents in Namibia are known to be sponsoring the foundation. Obviously not short of funds, Kerina in October 1977 bought a farm for $135,000 and paid the first $65,000 in cash.

Pro-SWA produces a monthly magazine entitled "Times of Namibia" which actively promotes the South African–created and funded Turnhalle conference, now renamed the Democratic Turnhalle Alliance. Its contents are a rehash of articles that have previously appeared in newspapers and journals which support South Africa. It carries ads for ficticious companies which aim to hoodwink and defraud desperate businessmen who are looking for ways of making safe their investments in Namibia.

South African businessmen have recently been called upon to take a more active role in helping to sell South African policy overseas. Suggestions include the holding of shareholders' meetings and seminars outside the country and the sponsoring of trade missions. But even former British Chancellor of the Exchequer, Mr. Reginald Maudling, found this hard to stomach. Speaking at a seminar held in Pretoria to discuss South Africa's international image, he was forced to point out that "You cannot blackmail us into supporting what we believe to be wrong."

As South Africa's propaganda campaign is linked to big business, so is it also a primary element in its military strategy. Earlier this year secret documents detailing South African Defence Force instructions on psychological warfare came into SWAPO's hands from a South African soldier who had just completed his military service. One document, entitled "Guide to Psychological Warfare," and intended for South African army officers, defines psychological action as consisting of "the application of various coordinated measures . . . initiated for the purpose of influencing opinion, feelings, beliefs, and thus attitudes and behavior of neutrals, allies and adversaries."

Peaceful forms of resistance to the South African regime are lumped together with the armed struggle and this is used as a justification for the use of armed force against peaceful resistance such as strikes and demonstrations. Churches and church organizations are regarded as part of "the enemy." Indeed South Africa's anti-SWAPO campaign has also been directed against the churches in Namibia which have long supported the cause of Namibian liberation. South Africa accuses the churches of being puppets of SWAPO. One leaflet distributed in northern Namibia depicts President Nujoma urinating on a church. (There is a saying in Ovambo that if you urinate in someone's ear, you control that person.)

The "Guide to Psychological Warfare" shows South Africa's concern with the flagging morale of its own troops. Increasing numbers of South Africans are leaving the country to avoid military service in Namibia. That a South African soldier passed on these documents to SWAPO is sufficient testimony to the increasing demoralization of the South African army. Meanwhile the South Africans are calling for personal sacrifices from their troops in the fight to the death for what they know to be "right."

South Africa's propaganda offensive in northern Namibia is a blatant attempt to confuse the Namibian people and to shake their revolutionary commitment so that it can continue to rule Namibia illegally and exploit our human and natural resources. But South Africa's inhuman oppression and ruthless exploitation have so deepened our people's revolutionary commitment that no amount of propaganda will deflect them from their cause.

The South African army has chosen as its watchword "Vas-byt" (Vigilance). Let our watchword be "VICTORY!" In the words of the Secretary for SWAPO's Women's Council within Namibia:

We are armed with the most dangerous and efficient weapons with which to wage the struggle: our loudspeakers are our cannons, our tongues the AK 47, and our ammunition is the truth.

The Women Militants

**Woman militant
receives award - LSM photo**

*In the following interview, Netumbo Nandi, Deputy Representative of SWAPO in Zambia and member of the movement's Central Committee, and Mathilda Amoomo, Secretary in SWAPO's Defense Office, discuss the particular situation of Namibian women under colonialism and within the liberation struggle. The interview was conducted in October 1976 by Carole Collins, a member of the Chicago Committee for African Liberation and was originally published under the title **This is the Time: Interview with Two Namibian Women** in 1977. Our version is extracted from the original.*

Mathilda, where do you come from in Namibia and what were some of the problems you faced?

Mathilda: I am from the same area as comrade Netumbo, the northern part of Namibia, near the Angolan border. For the married Namibian rural women, much of their married life is spent in separation from their husbands. The longest time a married contract worker can stay with his family at home is about four months before he returns for 12 to 18 more months away on contract.

When the men are away for a year or more on contract the wives and daughters have to assume so many family responsibilities without the cheering help of their husbands and mature sons or cousins. For example, there is a severe shortage of clinics and hospitals in the rural areas. Malaria is always endemic among children in these areas, especially during the wet, rainy seasons. Although the rainy season is when people should spend much of their time cultivating their fields, more often than not you find women flocking with their children on their backs to far distant clinics in search of scarce medical services.

In these rural areas, then, is it the women who do most of the agricultural work?

Mathilda: Yes. You find that apart from something like a one-hour break at about 10 a.m. to go for breakfast to feed the children, women in these areas work in the fields from 5 a.m. to 1 p.m. from Monday to Saturday, every week. This is true whether you are talking about cultivation, weeding or harvesting seasons of the year. The men help when they are not on contract, except for threshing and grinding grain for flour, which is women's work.

After spending up to seven hours of backbreaking labor in the fields, women in the rural areas do not retire to rest for the day. They must also fetch water, grind grain into flour, and prepare meals, not to mention washing the babies and their diapers. I do not mean to suggest that our men do nothing at all. They cut and clear trees off the fields for cultivation, and dig wells to obtain drinking water for both people and animals. They look after the herds. But on the whole, these are far less energy-taking duties when compared to those performed by women.

LIFE UNDER COLONIALISM—WOMEN IN TOWNS

We've talked mostly about Namibian women in rural areas. Can you tell us what life is like for women in towns and cities under colonial rule?

Netumbo: German and South African settlers took away the people's land and livestock in the southern and central parts of Namibia where most of the towns are located today. Both African men and women in these areas were reduced to the level of a dispossessed laboring class. The central and southern parts of Namibia have been more intensely affected by white colonial settlement than those areas in the north. Evicted from their land, the people in these areas had to work on ranching estates of the colonial settlers, the men looking after the settlers' herds and the women working as domestic servants.

So towns developed and more women were drawn into the domestic service of the colonial settlers, working for mere subsistence wages. In most cases there was not even the question of wages. Women working as servants could obtain no wages but would be paid in terms of food and clothing handouts. This was the situation in the early days of colonial rule, especially during the German period.

Western corporate monopolies came to Namibia in order to extract minerals. There emerged a rapid process of extensive mining activity. This meant that a large percentage of the Namibian men entered the labor force through contract labor in the mines. The women were left to do domestic service in the rapidly expanding towns. Whereas it was possible for the men who worked in the mining, construction and fishing industries for many years to become at least semi-skilled workers, it has been virtually impossible for women working in domestic service to acquire any kind of productive skills. The situation has not fundamentally changed since the days of German colonialism.

Neither the German nor the South African colonial regimes ever really bothered to establish institutions of learning for Africans which would have enabled Namibian women to acquire trades or professional skills. The only professional women you can find in Namibia's towns are nurses and teachers. But nearly all the women teachers are primary school level, which means that they are at the lowest scale of pay. The same is true with respect to nursing.

Urban women are slightly better off than rural women. The majority of urban women have at least a chance to get the rudiments of formal schooling. So most of the urban women are either literate or semi-literate. There are at least one or two "Bantu"* primary schools in most of the major towns, whereas in the rural areas there are many villages or districts which have no schools. So a good number of rural women have never sat under the roof of a classroom in their life.

Since women generally do not participate in most of the key industries, such as mining, construction and transport, there is a comparatively high percentage of unemployed women in Namibian towns. The only industries which employ a small number of women are fishing and packing industries. You might find a few women working in fish canning factories at places like Walvis Bay and Luderitz Bay, Namibia's two most important centers of fishing industry. In places like Windhoek, the capital of Namibia, you might also find a few women working in the meat-packing industry.

Most of the lower professional jobs such as bank teller, secretary or clerk/typist are essentially reserved for white women in Namibia; and there are no trade schools to provide African women in the towns with skills.

What is the average wage of a woman doing domestic work?

Netumbo: Women working in domestic service in the towns on the average would earn 10–15 Rand per month. ($10–15)

SWAPO MOBILIZES WOMEN

You are both women who have become involved in the struggle for national liberation. Could you tell us about women's participation in SWAPO and what particular problems you face in mobilizing other women?

---

* "Bantu" is the term used by the ruling white Afrikaaner regime to refer to Africans. "Bantu Education" is a system of education adopted by the Afrikaaner Nationalist Party in 1954, designed to train Africans only for the lowest levels of labor.

Netumbo: In the early stages of SWAPO, the participation of women was small, due to the lingerings of semi-feudal mentality and social structure in the country. Women suffer from an inferiority complex that is centuries old and deeply ingrained, which tends to make women afraid to speak in public at meetings and to participate in decision-making processes. So the movement was dealing with not only general lack of organizational experience, but also a lack of self-confidence among women. We were basing ourselves on our old traditions that a woman is a woman, and as such, her place was in the kitchen. Against this background, the involvement of women in the struggle was relatively slow compared to that of our male comrades.

I must point out, however, that hundreds of Namibian women did participate in the historic Windhoek uprising of December, 1959, involving mass boycotts of public works, transport, cinema and beer halls in protest against the colonial regime's arbitrary removal of Windhoek's old African township to a new site which was located much farther away from town. Several women were among the 11 shot dead and 50 wounded. The Windhoek uprising represents an important point of departure in the history of our national liberation struggle. It marked the shift from the policies of petitioning the UN to that of mass agitation. In short, I can say women were slower than the men to get involved in the early years, but they were not very far behind because they too felt the oppression as much as the men.

How did SWAPO try to mobilize women in the early stages of the organization?

Netumbo: In the 1970's women began to take a very active part in organizing meetings and rallies. We began to see that when SWAPO youth activists held meetings and demonstrations against colonialism, girls were sometimes in the majority. Some of the men began to rethink their traditional prejudices against women, as a good number of women began to be vocal at meetings. Colonial jails also began to be filled not only with men but also with women. When the South African government ordered mass public floggings of people's naked bodies in 1973, nearly half of the victims were women. Over the last two years thousands of Namibians decided to enlist in the People's Liberation Army of Namibia; a considerable number are women. Today you will find women at nearly every level of our movement's structure. But whatever has been achieved so far must be seen not only as a victory against the existing social and economic structure which discriminates against women in employment and education, but also as a victory against the prejudices among some of our male comrades.

What obstacles have you experienced as women as you participate in the struggle for national liberation?

Netumbo: At the organizational level obstacles to the participation of women are rarely ever noticeable nowadays; maybe you will find them on a personal basis. But on a personal basis they are not so effective as they could have been at organizational levels. For over half a decade now, women have been playing a very active role in SWAPO. Women have been participating in meetings and in elections. Some have distinguished themselves as being able public speakers, organizers and chairpersons. So, in the process, many more women have begun to realize that being able to do serious political work is not the monopoly of men. Similarly, many more male comrades have been able to overcome their feelings of male superiority.

In many struggles, women have found that men's attitudes have been an obstacle to their full participation. Has this been your experience too and if so, how have you overcome it?

Netumbo: In the course of our struggle, the male comrades' attitudes were also an obstacle to one degree or another. Little was expected of women's contribution. But this obstacle was taken up by the women themselves when they started to demonstrate their capabilities in performing their duties equally well as did their male comrades.

What are some of the activities of the SWAPO Women's Council?

Netumbo: The establishment of the Women's Council inside Namibia was a very difficult undertaking, as were all other anti-colonial political activities. The Council tried by all means to organize women in small meetings. A lot of effort had to be made to encourage women to participate more in SWAPO programs, such as those concerned with public meetings and demonstrations. All these provided occasions for educating the Namibian women politically. Consequently, it became apparent by 1972 that quite a good number of women were becoming very active. When, for instance, the United Nations Secretary General, Dr. Kurt Waldheim and his personal representative, Dr. Alfred Escher, visited Namibia on different occasions in 1972, women came out in impressive numbers to urge the UN to take immediate and serious measures to assist the Namibian people to attain their national liberation.

By 1973, the South African colonial jails in Namibia were getting filled with SWAPO activists, including many women. This was basically a result of the politicizing work of both the SWAPO Women's Council and the Youth League. Today, you will find that in every district, municipality or village where there is a SWAPO branch, there is a Women's Council representative who is charged with the specific responsibility of organizing and politicizing women.

THE FUTURE OF WOMEN IN NAMIBIA

What are the future tasks of the Women's Council in the struggle for national liberation?

Netumbo: The immediate objective of SWAPO is the achievement of national independence. Its ultimate aim is the establishment of a truly free, democratic and classless society in Namibia. We have not even reached the first and most immediate objective yet. This always makes us aware of not becoming complacent with whatever accomplishments we might have made. But as we have been trying to show, the SWAPO Women's Council has succeeded in drawing thousands of Namibian women into our liberation activity. This liberation activity is in itself an important process of learning. It has exposed thousands of Namibian women to many new ideas which are revolutionizing their world outlook.

There are many things which remain to be done to mobilize women in the struggle for national and social liberation. The Council is striving constantly to raise the level of the Namibian women's political consciousness to ensure that the right of Namibia's women to participate fully in all political, cultural, social and productive activities of our society, is always at the center of policy decisions. It is only when the women themselves are armed with a high level of political consciousness that our movement can guarantee that reactionary ideas such as male chauvinism and female docility will have no place in a liberated Namibia.

The
Price
Of
Liberation

drawing by
Selma Waldman

Following is an excerpt from the life history of SWAPO militant, *HINANANJE SHAFODINO NEHOVA. Born into a peasant family in southern Angola, Nejova frequently visited relatives in Namibia as his people, the Kwanyamas—one of the seven sub-groups which comprise the larger Ovambo group—inhabit both sides of the Angola-Namibia border. Under colonial influence, Nehova's parents abandoned the traditional customs and adopted Christianity. His father, a catechist, assisted the Portuguese clergy.*

Certain benefits accrued to Nehova as a result of his family's cultural and personal ties with the Portuguese. After learning to read at home, he went to a mission school where he did quite well. In school, however, Nehova gained deeper insight into Portuguese methods.

"We were not allowed to speak our own language. Every morning Father Nazarre would punish students for speaking Oshikwanyama, beating them with a palmatoria. The palmatoria was very painful indeed. It is full of holes and when you get hit it sucks up the blood. If we refused this punishment, the father would put small stones on the floor and force us to kneel on them during the whole class.

"The Europeans ate different food than the African students. They always had meat and rice while we ate porridge. I was aware of this because I was in charge of serving their table. I sometimes got leftovers, bones, soup and so on, but one father, Joao Batista, purposely put cigarette ashes in his food so that we couldn't eat it."

After completing primary school in 1963, Nehova taught school for a year before entering secondary school at Seminario de Jau, near the town of Sa da Bandeira. These were years of increasing political activity in Southern Africa: Lumumba's example in the Congo shook the foundations of the colonial regimes, anti-colonial revolts had begun in northern Angola, and the Ovamboland People's Organization, SWAPO's forerunner, was recruiting on both sides of the Namibian border. With these developments came increased Portuguese and South African repression. Nehova became involved in the political activism erupting at Seminario de Jau nd was consequently expelled. In 1967, to avoid being drafted into the colonial army, he went to Namibia.

By the violent appropriation of African land, the South African regime has divided Namibia into two regions. The fertile and mineral-rich heartlands constitute the "Police Zone." No African can own land in this area and only those Blacks who are needed as workers in the White-run economy can live there—and then only in the specially designated "locations" or "compounds."

The bulk of the African population has been driven into the other *region, the barren reservations—or "homelands"—which circle the Police Zone. With few other means of subsistence, the men are forced to seek employment as "contract workers" with the Whites. On contract the African worker is at the complete mercy of his employers and the colonial regime; he will be imprisoned for changing his job or trying to quit before the contract expires. Wages are miserable as are conditions of work. The contract labor system amounts to nothing less than slavery adapted to capitalist relations of production and has earned the bitter hatred of all Namibians.*

Having escaped from Angola, Nehova worked for some time in the northern region of Ovamboland before entering St. Mary's secondary school where he met Thomas Kamati and other leaders-to-be of the SWAPO Youth League. Nehova soon joined SWAPO. Following a demonstration to demand Namibian independence, he was again expelled from school with hundreds of other students. . . .

The Walvis Bay Strike

After my expulsion from St. Mary's, I went to Odibo where I met three friends from school, Thomas Kamati, Ndaxu Namolo and Philip Hainana. They had just arrived from Walvis Bay where they had been working in the canneries. We discussed what should be done next, as many students had been expelled and were forced to flee police repression. This is when we decided to go south to the industrial areas of Namibia, particularly Walvis Bay. We intended to mobilize workers for a general strike that was being planned.

While we were at Odibo, my brother Stevao came from home on his first visit to Namibia. He had saved some money and offered to pay for our journey to Walvis Bay. We stayed at Odibo for about two weeks before going on to Ondangua, where we found another schoolmate, Nabo Nafidi, who was also heading for Walvis Bay. An acquaintance of mine who worked in the offices of the South West African Native Labor Association (SWANLA),* managed to get us travel documents. He made passes for people going into the Police Zone for holidays or even business. They were simple papers which he wrote and stamped with the official stamp. With these we took a lift to the Onamutune checkpoint where the police check people to make sure they have the proper documents. One of the European officers looked at my passport.

---

* The agency that coordinates the recruiting and transport of contract workers to the farms and industries of the Police Zone.

"Do you want to travel with this?"

"Yes."

He looked at me, "Yes, who?"

"Yes, you!"

"No, you must say 'Yes, Baas' because you are a kaffir and I am a South African. I am white. You must always answer, 'Yes, Baas.'"

But I insisted, "No, you are not my boss. I don't work for you and you don't give me money."

"So, you are one of *those* Kaffirs; from Odibo or Onguediva. OK, you can go."

We drove on to Tsumeb where we spent the night in the house of Namolo's father. Namolo and my brother stayed there to help others in Ovamboland get passes while the rest of us continued to Walvis Bay.

Nabo and I left first, spending the whole day and night on the train. We arrived in Walvis Bay at 6 a.m. From the Station we went directly to the contract workers' compound but, as we had no permits, we had to wait for some friends to finish work in order to borrow their passes. We stayed in the compound until Namolo, Kamati and Stevao arrived a week later.

Walvis Bay is a small town. The Europeans live on the coastal side of town and the Africans further inland, into the desert. The distance between them is about half a mile. The compound of the Ovambo contract workers is very big. At that time there were only about seven thousand workers, but usually there are ten thousand or more. Most of them work in the factories, the building industry, or on the railway. A wall surrounds several buildings where the men live twelve to a room. The bunks are made of cement and just banged against the wall, three high. There is a kitchen and a beer hall built by the government. There is also a soccer field. The rooms have no heat and at night can get quite cold. Sometimes it even snows. The police used to come around to check passes. However, we didn't have any trouble as we always carried our borrowed passes.

After we had settled in, we went to find work. But everywhere they asked us for work permits which, of course, we didn't have. We therefore had to forge some papers with a stamp stolen from Augostineum College in Windhoek. We presented these to factory managers, saying we were students on holiday looking for work. Finally, we were hired at the Ovenstone fish cannery.*

---

* Ovenstone products are imported and sold in North America by Del Monte.

I was made a "coffee boy." I served the office staff coffee and delivered mail. The managers were generally OK; they were American, British and German. This job gave me the opportunity to read newspapers and magazines, but sometimes this made me look suspicious. The staff didn't know I spoke English and thinking I couldn't understand, often criticized me in my presence. They would say, "He looks like an agitator; he has a beard and reads newspapers." So I had to watch my step.

During the second week in Walvis Bay we had a meeting with students from Windhoek to discuss our plans for a strike. SWAPO members from Walvis Bay were also present. Just about every student was a SWAPO member even though you couldn't come right out and say it. We all attended regular SWAPO meetings twice a week.

Soon we began to organize. We would approach one or two workers in each factory, in the railway and building companies. We only talked to those we trusted. All agreed that something had to be done about the contract labor system.

Around that time the South African Commissioner-General for Indigenous People wrote a newspaper article saying the contract workers wanted to work under the system. He said the workers came to the government and asked for jobs, never complaining that the system was inhuman. We used this article to tell our fellow workers: "See, the South Africans are saying that we are pleased with this system, so we should do something to show them that we really don't want it. If we break this system with a strike, we could have the freedom to choose our jobs and move freely around the country; to take our families with us and to visit our friends wherever they are." Everyone supported these ideas.

In the beginning of November we held a meeting on the town soccer field. About six thousand workers from every section of Walvis Bay attended. Chipala Mokaxua, Namolo, Kamati, I and many others addressed the crowd, all saying that we should lay down our tools and go back home. We said the government had no right to interfere with our wages and that we did not need the Labor Association. We also denounced the chiefs for helping the South Africans organize the system.

The reaction after the speeches was overwhelming and support for the strike swelled. We also voted to send delegates or letters to workers in other parts of Namibia, like Oranjemund, Luderitz, Windhoek, Grootfontein, Tsumeb and the farming districts to tell them that on December 11 we dould go on strike, leave for Ovamboland

and tell the chiefs that we would no longer work under the contract system.

After this meeting fourteen of the speakers, all of them our friends, were arrested and the police began searching for Kamati and myself. They were trying to stop the organizing by imprisoning the leaders. Fortunately, they did not know what we looked like. We had to go under false names and at night slept in the fishing boats or the seaman's mission where the police wouldn't suspect us. Even the African informers did not know who we were. When they arrested Namolo, Kamati was actually sleeping on the same bed but he was so small and boyish-looking that they weren't even suspicious of him.

I can still remember the time when the police entered a house we were visiting. They approached us, looked at Kamati and said:

"We are looking for a person called Thomas Kamati. He used to live in the location* but we don't know what he looks like."

Kamati answered: "Oh, Thomas Kamati, you must mean the one who lives in number 12."

This was the Kamati who had previously been arrested by mistake.

"No, not that one, there is another Kamati around here somewhere."

"Oh well, we don't know that one."

Then they left without asking any more questions. We had a number of close calls. One morning while I was walking to the factory I was stopped by the police and asked where I was going.

"To work. I work in one of the factories."

"At this time? It's only five o'clock!"

"Yes."

"All right, get in."

I got into the car and we just drove around the town. They wanted to know where I was from. I told them I was born in Walvis Bay and had lived there all my life.

"Are you living in the town or the compound?"

"I'm from the location."

"What's your house number?"

I gave them a number off the top of my head and then told them I worked at Ovenstone. They must have believed me because I was

---

* The "location" is the part of town set aside for the local African families. It is always separate from the contract worker compounds.

driven to the factory and dropped off without further questioning. Except for times like this, we didn't have much to fear since the workers left the factories in large crowds and it was difficult for the police to single anyone out. Nonetheless, they still asked individuals for passes and questioned them about the strike leaders. Despite this intimidation, we managed to talk to the workers one by one, convincing them that the only way to improve our living and working conditions was to strike.

Two days before the strike, Kamati, Namolo and I sent a letter to the Commissioner-General of the Indigenous Peoples, the Administrator for Namibia and Prime Minister Vorster explaining our disagreement with the newspaper article the Commissioner-General had written. We told them that they would soon witness our true feelings about the contract labor system. Shortly after, the South African government called a meeting of workers to which the headmen of seven Namibian tribes and Bishop Awala were invited to speak in an attempt to convince them not to strike. But when the headmen took the microphone, they were shouted down. Only Bishop Awala spoke, saying that, in his way, he, too, was trying to change the system.

Someone spoke from the crowd: "Look, our brothers have been arrested and now the white administrators are trying to stop our strike. The Administrator tells us he is considering the matter but wants to talk with the Ovamboland authorities first. They are cheating us! All they really want to do is arrest our leaders and continue the system."

"All right," he answered, right in the presence of the Special Branch agents who were recording the meeting, "then you have no choice but to go on strike."

The crowd burst into shouting and applause, breaking up the meeting with SWAPO songs. Those who had passes burned them in further protest.

At the same time, the delegates we had sent to Windhoek, Tsumeb, Swakopmund, and elsewhere returned with reports from all over the country that the news had been received with great enthusiasm. The workers in Windhoek and some miners in that area had decided to join the strike immediately. There was great solidarity among the African people. In Walvis Bay, many of those living in the town entered the compound. Even people not working under the contract system came to stay in the compound. Others gave good to the workers going on strike.

The next day, Monday, December 10th, we informed our bosses

that we were leaving for Ovamboland because of our opposition to the contract labor system. Some of the British and American workers supported us. One of them told me: "You must do what you have decided. If you keep quiet and don't do anything, the companies will do nothing to improve your conditions. You must hit them and only then will they change. And if you find some people vacillating, stop them!"

When we returned to the compound after work, we found it surrounded by armed police. They did not try to prevent us from entering or leaving; they didn't even check our passes. They just sat quietly and watched us pack our things. The next morning there were trucks waiting outside to take us to the trains. The government provided this transportation because they were afraid there might be trouble. Rumors had been circulating that we planned to set the compound on fire and that we were going to attack the Whites in town. So they had decided not to try to break the strike by force. About five thousand workers left that morning, singing as they marched to the trucks. Managers and journalists were there to watch, but the police prevented them from getting close. The journalists were not allowed to take pictures. Those who tried had their cameras taken away, the film removed and some were even arrested.

Kamati and I did not leave with this group. Some of the workers had not been paid for three months and it had been decided that they should stay on the job and leave for Ovamboland only after they had been paid. Fearing they might become demoralized and betray the others, we stayed to encourage them. We spread leaflets throughout the compound and even in the location. But this became increas- for two weeks because of the police searches.

The government attempted to bring in scabs from outside Namibia. This, however, was a total failure. The work was too hard for them and they didn't have the necessary skills. They were also intimidated by the other workers. Some of the employers even refused to hire them. After a while, most simply asked to be returned to where they came from.

The strike began to spread all over the country. The South Africans had made the mistake of announcing it over the radio and this alone had caused a great many workers to leave for Ovamboland. Even small boys working on farms had left their jobs. Within one week, twenty-five industrial centers were hit by the strike. The only place where there were problems was Oranjemund, where the "Baas-Boys," who are paid better than average, had great influence. So only three thousand of the five thousand Oranjemund workers left. But everywhere else, on the farms, in the mines, in the factories, the walk-out was nearly total.

Kamati and I kept in touch with what was going on by listening to the radio and reading newspapers. We couldn't move freely but a number of times we managed to telephone comrades in Ovamboland. They also used to write and keep us up-to-date on developments there. A few days after their arrival, the people were made aware of the strikers' demands at a large meeting. The chiefs and headmen were told that the strike would last until the whole system changed. News of the workers' return and the strike's objectives spread across Ovamboland, escalating into many violent acts against the authorities and their collaborators. Many collaborators were beaten and some of the most hated were killed. A great deal of their property was destroyed.

As these activities became widespread, the strikers started more serious actions. For instance, when a headman named Kalengi, who feared reprisals from the people for his collaboration with the South Africans, called the police for protection, they were ambushed by workers with spears and bows. Many people were killed on both sides. We also heard that the strikers had begun to tear down the fence separating Namibia from Angola; in one day five hundred kilometers of fencing between Okovango and the Cunene River was destroyed.

Around this time we sent one of our comrades in Walvis Bay, an MPLA militant, to Ovamboland to report on the developments. Through him we learned that the strike and other actions had spread into southern Angola. More than half of the contract workers in Namibia were from Angola and had returned home with the same intentions as those in Ovamboland. Many symbols of colonial rule were attacked by the strikers and support rose among the people of the area. The situation became so critical that reinforcements of Portuguese troops were sent down from Luanda. At last, when the authorities at Ondjiva felt unable to contain the strikers, a meeting was called between the Governor and the population. People came from all areas of southern Angola, and most of them were armed. The Governor arrived with an additional convoy of troops and simply tried to threaten the people into submission. But the reaction of the crowd was so violent that he had to change his attitude and listen to the people's demands which centered mainly around unjust taxes and restrictions on Africans owning land. The Governor listened to the demands and promised to return to Lisbon to convince his government of the need to change. But his promises only acted to relax the people's vigilance and left them open to attacks by the Portuguese troops and PIDE.* Many of the leaders were arrested, including my brother Stevao, who had returned with the strikers from Walvis Bay and become one of the main mobilizers. Many of those arrested were later killed by PIDE in Ondjiva prison.

The same type of situation developed in Namibia. In February, all the headmen in the country met at Oshikate and came out in support of the strikers. This was followed almost immediately by another meeting in Swakopmund which included the Commissioner-General and the Minister for Ovambo Education. The strike leaders in Ovamboland asked permission to take part because changes in the contract system were being discussed but were refused.

We were not represented at all. The South Africans promised many changes in working conditions and salaries, but when the workers returned, the system remained almost exactly the same. Some wages rose slightly but all other changes were simply outweighed by new restrictions and forms of authority.

When the workers saw that things remained basically the same, they started to strike again. However, many of those returning were new, replacing workers who had been arrested. They lacked experienced leadership. Organization among the workers, therefore, was much weaker. Furthermore, the police began to use force: workers were attacked with guns and tear gas. As people were simultaneously being rounded up and jailed in Ovamboland, many of the workers were intimidated. Thus the strike ended in early March.

TO THE BOTSWANA BORDER

Kamati and I realized that we could not stay in Walvis Bay. It was impossible to appear in the open and seemed only a matter of time before we were caught. Many others had been arrested and the jail was full. There was no reason for us to remain, so we decided to escape through Angola to Zambia, or into Botswana to join the liberation movement. Four of us were to go, Kamati and I and two others involved in organizing, Jack Hidimwa and Valiho Haita.

Most people escaping through Botswana got the necessary travel information from comrades in Windhoek: how to get trains, which were the safest routes, and what to avoid while traveling. We divided into two groups and headed for Windhoek by train. Hidimwa and I

---

* The Portuguese secret police.

left first. From the Ovenstone factory, I had stolen some papers bearing the company seal. We used these to obtain travel permits. We got to Windhoek without problems and contacted some friends who lived in the location. They gave us money because we had left nearly everything we owned behind to avoid drawing suspicion. Our friends advised us on the best way to leave the country. Waiting until dark to buy our tickets, we took a train to Gobabis which is near the Botswana border. The European at the ticket counter was no problem, but on the train many people watched us. We were wearing jeans and carrying bags which were not commonly used in that area, so people may have suspected us. Arriving in Gobabis at six the following morning, we jumped off the train and vanished into the bush; the police in Gobabis were very active and had arrested many people trying to reach the border.

It was impossible to go into town, so we headed through the bush to the African location where we could get food and water. The food situation was not very good but we filled our bags with water and set off on foot for Sandfontein, the border station a hundred and seven kilometers from Gobabis. We stayed in the bush, walking beside the road until it forked. Not knowing which way to go, we guessed and followed the road to the left. But this turned out to be the road to Omounga and after walking two days, we were a long way from Sandfontein. Our water ran out and we did not have much food left. We thought of going to one of the farms we passed but this would have been very dangerous because of the Boers. So we kept walking and finally ran into a Bushman who spoke Afrikaans. He worked on a Boer farm but since the owner was away, we were able to get food and water. He explained that we were three days from the border and pointed out the direction.

We set off again. The country here was very desolate, mostly desert with large mounds of sand and few small bushes. It was very hot and without food and water it was not long before we were very weak and tired. We had to stop frequently in order to rest. Our feet were cut and swollen from walking; even our armpits began to swell because of the heat and lack of water. We often passed places where there was water, but the police and Boers were always present.

It was not until we came across another Bushman who told us we were still far from Sandfontein that we decided to enter one of the farms. Africans always work on these farms and we hoped to get food and water from them without being seen by the owner. We were simply too hungry and tired to go any further. Early in the morning we entered a farm and managed to get across two fences and near the buildings. As it turned out, the Africans had left because the owner did not pay them well. He expected trouble and had placed police guards around the farm. Two guards in a tree watched us approach. They called out for us to stop and came over with a dog. There was one European and an African who translated for him.

"Where are you going, are you on your way to Botswana?"

"No, we are going to Sandfontein to see our employer."

"Where are you coming from then?"

We had passed a number of farms the previous night and so I just gave them one of the names.

"We are from Voltrius farm."

"Ah yes, are you Hereros or Ovambos?"

"We are Hereros."

"OK, you can go, this is the way to Sandfontein."

He pointed off in a direction away from the farm. We had just started to leave when another policeman came up and said, "Get them back here, tell those two *kaffirs** I want to see them." When we heard this we started moving faster but the African policeman ran over and told us his boss wanted to speak with us. I said we didn't have the time and turned to leave. He let us go but soon we heard a car coming in our direction. We tried to run though we were too tired to get far. We hid in some bushes but they had a dog and so discovered us without much trouble. We were surrounded and ordered to get in the car. When we drove back to the farm, they phoned the police station at Sandfontein. Within ten minutes a jeep pulled up with a South African policeman and an African agent. As soon as he saw us, the African said that we were not Hereros but Ovambo troublemakers trying to leave the country.

They drove us to Gobabis where we admitted that we were not Hereros. "We are actually from Walvis Bay. We were students at Onguediva, but were expelled and have decided to continue our education in Botswana." However, when they searched our bags, they found our SWAPO cards in between some books.

"Aha, so you are terrorists. You were on you way to join up with SWAPO."

"No, no. We are interested in SWAPO, yes, but we are not terrorists."

The police didn't believe us and we were put in a prison. It was

---

* South African equivalent of "nigger."

overcrowded, dirty and the beds were full of lice. The food was mostly porridge and sometimes dog or hyena meat which made us vomit.

We waited two days before being interrogated again. A white South African officer who had been in Ovamboland during the strike confronted us.

"I have been informed by the judge at Onguediva that you did not want to study, that you just wanted to stir up trouble. So now, you *kaffirs*, tell me, how did you organize the strike? Who helped you? Were Maxuiriri and Meroro involved?"

"We didn't organize it, we just took part; it was a general strike," I protested. He just looked at us coldly and said nothing else. Finally, they took us back to our cells. The next day they took us out again but we were separated this time. I was taken to the same officer who had since discovered that I was from Angola. He was sitting behind a desk and an African sergeant stood against the door behind me."

"Are you a member of the MPLA?"

"No," I answered, "I know nothing about MPLA."

"Yes you do, because you belong to SWAPO, and being an Angolan you are in this country illegally. You were going for military training and we'll lay charges on that basis, Now, things would be a lot easier if you would tell me who told you to organize the Onguediva demonstration and the Walvis Bay strike."

"But I didn't organize the strike. I just took part like everyone else."

He looked at me. "All right, you are lying. I will simply have to force it out of you."

He called for another African policeman who brought in a small machine with wires hanging from it and plugged it into the wall. I was handcuffed, blindfolded and pushed onto the floor; my hands were tied to the wires.

The South African was swearing. "If you don't tell me the truth, you goddam *kaffir*, you'll regret it. We'll make you shit in your pants! Who told you to organize the strike?"

I remained silent. Suddenly a shock ran through my fingers, up my arms and shook my whole body. It was terrible. I felt pain all over my body but my head was the worst. It was like an explosion in my brain. They kept turning it on and off, on and off, lashing me about the head and shoulders with a whip and shouting obscenities. It was unbelievable. The South African continued asking me about the strike.

"Who sent you to live in the country? Was it Maxuiriri?"

They kept this up for several hours. I didn't lose consciousness or give up. The pain was tremendous, but after a while the electricity seemed to make everything go numb. Finally, they dragged me back to a cell.

After three weeks of interrogation, solitary confinement and torture, I discovered that Kamati and Valiho had also been caught. I learned from one of the African guards that they too had been accused of terrorism and were going through the same ordeal. In the end they must have believed part of our story because we were only charged for not having proper travel papers. After being sentenced to three months of solitary, we weren't tortured but were sometimes interrogated by police from Pretoria. We spent these three months just waiting; no work, no walks, no exercise at all. The days seemed very long and one month felt like three.

IN THE HANDS OF PIDE

When our time was up, we were taken to Oshikate in Ovamboland. Kamati and the others were handed over to the headman, while I was to be given to the Portuguese. We said goodbye and were separated. I was very sad. I didn't think I would ever see them again. I had tried not to think about it in solitary, but I was sure the Portuguese would either kill me or send me to Sao Nicolau, the prison for liberation movement militants. I knew the PIDE agents would try to squeeze information out of me and probably kill me once I was no longer useful.

I arrived at the PIDE headquarters in the Ondjiva (Pereira de Eca) prison during July 1972. Silva Texeira, the chief inspector of the Cunene Branch, began to interrogate me immediately.

"What were you going to do in Zambia?"

I thought he was just confused. "I wasn't going to Zambia, I was on my way to Botswana."

But again he asked, "*What* were you going to do in *Zambia*?"

I thought it best to go along with him. "I was going for further study."

"Further study! Don't we have schools here in Angola?"

I remained silent.

"Ah yes, the school of terrorism, I forgot. And there's been a lot of development with this school in Zambia hasn't there?"

He then ordered one of the other officers to take me away, saying as I left: "You'll eventually tell us the truth about everything we want to know about SWAPO and MPLA. If you do, you shall go free; if not, well, you'll be around for a long time. And believe me, you won't enjoy it."

I was thrown onto the floor of a cell. Still handcuffed from my arrival, I found it difficult to move. They splashed water onto the floor, which made it very cold, and refused to give me any blankets.

"Terrorists don't need blankets. Why, even those in the bush don't have blankets, so you can do without."

The cell was small and dark; no windows, just a hole in the iron door.

I spent two days without food before the door opened again. An officer came in, asked if I was with MPLA, then beat me with a whip when I said no. It was incredibly painful and went on for so long that he became exhausted and had to be replaced. I was bleeding all over. Finally, after what seemed like hours, I passed out. When I regained consciousness my whole body was swollen; my head ached and I was still bleeding.

The next day I was returned to the office. They had gathered information about my Walvis Bay and student activities. This changed their attitude toward me somewhat; I can remember Texeira saying after one interrogation:

"You are a man who is determined to do something but can really do nothing. You have an idea in your head which can't be released."

They decided to get more information about me so I was left alone for a while. During this time I saw many prisoners tortured. The hole in my door gave me a good view of the interrogation office but sometimes they did it deliberately in front of me. They would beat a man unconscious, bring him into my cell and say, "If you don't smarten up, we'll do the same to you."

During this time, a young Portuguese officer came in, explaining that he had fought against the nationalist movements in northern Angola. He told me that the movements were completely divided and fighting among themselves. "Look," he said, "Angola is a country with many tribal differences and the people are illiterate. If the Portuguese left, there would be civil war." He also talked about the movement leaders, saying that Agostinho Neto, Amilcar Cabral and Sam Nujoma had been good men when they started, but had been corrupted once they went abroad. These leaders, he claimed, were living with white prostitutes while the guerrillas were starving in the bush. Although I knew little about these things, I did not believe him and thought he was just trying to convince me either to give him information or denounce the liberation movements. I was given cigarettes and a week to think about giving information. They always tried to bribe me with my freedom, even offering me prostitutes and a good life in Luanda. But I never said anything; so the torture began again.

One day they took me into a room I had not seen before. The walls and floor were stained with blood and a guard was holding a machine gun. As we entered, the officer said this was my last chance to talk. I thought I was going to die; you know, I was relieved! I had reached the point where the interrogations and torture had become too much. I was tired, very tired and wanted it all to end. I preferred to die. I was stood up against a concreet wall chipped with bullet holes. Again the PIDE officer asked me to name MPLA militants operating in the area, and again I remained silent. He only asked me once and then said, "All right, have it your way. You have five minutes to think it over, then you'll be shot." He left and I just stood there thinking my life was over. I was so tired, hungry and weak. When he returned, I just stared at him and said nothing. He got extremely angry and screamed to the others to get me out of his sight. Of course, the torture would begin anew, but nonetheless, I gained a little satisfaction from this incident.

It was now August; I had been in prison for nearly two months. I was no longer beaten so much but saw many who were. One day they brought in a man accused of possessing a pistol. He was given an extremely vicious beating. When he collapsed, they would pick him up and start over. He was almost dead when they stopped. They dragged him over to my cell, opened the door and said, "Here, have some company." He was unconscious and in terrible shape. They beat him every day for four days, trying to make him talk. On the last day, they strung him up on the wall upside-down. He was crying while they beat him and I didn't think he could last. It was horrible. He looked over at me and said, "Ah, my brother, bye-bye." His eyes turned up and I realized he was dead. I felt sickened by it. They left him hanging for two days, saying it was a lesson for me.

This sort of thing happened continuously. When I think about it now, the torture of others was even more disturbing than my own. For they were not always men like myself. Many young boys and old men were beaten and killed. Once an old fellow was brought into my cell after having been beaten. PIDE agents asked him about MPLA and SWAPO. He was old and had had no contact with the movements. But because he couldn't tell them what they wanted to know, they stripped him, took a knife and cut off his penis. He remained conscious and the pain must have been great. He knew he was going to die because he was losing so much blood. There was nothing I could do. I felt so helpless. After he died, they just put him into a bag and carried him away to throw him into the Cunene River as they did all their victims.

I could not understand these PIDE officials' lack of humanity. They seemed to do it for pleasure. Most were convinced that the Portuguese would remain in power and that the black majority would never throw them out, so they didn't worry about their crimes. I often thought about these people and the things they did. It was difficult to answer why these white people were killing Africans. Some, only charged with harmless civil crimes, were killed by the PIDE. The Portuguese rounded up whole towns, children, old men and women, for questioning and kept them for days without food. I could not understand this. I tried, but it was impossible. Why were they so fond of killing, why so brutal and inhuman?

In February 1973, our cells were being painted, so thirty of us were taken to another cell in the center of the prison. As it turned out, the officers had left some bags of millet and twenty bottle of whisky in this cell. We waited until night and then started eating and drinking. Almost all of us got drunk and started shouting: "Come and take us out of this hell, you asses from Portugal"; "Go back to Portugal"; and so on. Then the police came in with guns and started to laugh, saying they would shoot us if we didn't keep quiet. When they went away, we began to beat on the door; some of us were dancing and yelling more insults. In the morning troops came and we were asked who had been the first to drink. We said we didn't know and they started beating us with whips right there in the cell. Four people were killed by this beating.

Later that month an eighteen-year-old boy was caught with a knife. PIDE officers brought him into my cell and explained that he was a terrorist. I was given a whip and told to beat him. Of course I did not beat him hard. So, one of the officers took the whip and said, "You must beat him like this." He beat me severely then gave me the whip again. This time I beat the boy until he collapsed. It was horrible; that night the boy was inhaling and exhaling extremely deeply and I feared he would die.

Conditions in the cells were very bad. We got one meal a day, often just slopped on the floor. But the worst part was being alone. I tried to remember Kamati and our times in Walvis Bay or my parents and village. But my mind would get confused. It was quite miserable and I was afraid I was losing my mind. The loneliness was worse than the beating because you never got used to it, it kept getting harder each day. I never actually thought of taking my own life, but once or twice I wished they had killed me. It would have been so much easier.

Many people were killed in 1973. One night just as we were falling asleep, I heard loud noises. Two handcuffed Africans were being brought into the prison. Texeira was beating them with a *kiri** and killed them right their. This kind of thing went on and on.

I began to lose my sight in December. When we were taken out for work one day (the first time in months), I noticed everything was blurred. I found a newspaper but could not read it. Later, I realized I couldn't see clearly through the hole in the door. I developed an ulcer that same year. Whenever I ate, the pain was intense. Only my occasional cigarettes made it feel a little better.

Another comrade was put in my cell around this time. It was good to have company. And, because my cell mate had only been imprisoned recently, he was able to give me information on the movements. He told me Guinea-Bissau was almost completely liberated and that FRELIMO was making tremendous advances in Mozambique. Whenever I came in contact with other prisoners we discussed these things. It helped us withstand hardship to think we might be liberated soon. It gave us hope.

*   *   *   *   *

The prison at Ondjiva opened its doors shortly after the Lisbon coup on 25 April 1974. Several of the PIDE agents who did not immediately leave the area were subsequently killed by the liberated prisoners and the enraged local population.

On his release, Nehova looked like "a wild animal." Two years of hair and beard growth combined with a change in pigmentation due to malnutrition and lack of sunlight ("My skin was almost yellow") scared people off as he staggered out of the prison, barely able to walk. After recuperating at his parents' home for a few weeks, he returned to Ondjiva where he organized a network to help the hundreds of Namibians entering Angola to reach Zambia. In late 1974, fearing South African raids into Angola, he too left for Zambia.

This story was recorded as Nehova was waiting to receive medical treatment. He is still unable to read, his ulcer periodically erupts in bleeding, and his brain may have sustained permanent damage. But despite his horrific prison experiences, he remains a soft-spoken and

---

* Stick; traditional African weapon.

sensitive person. His burning wish to join SWAPO's guerrilla forces stems more from his feeling that nobody should rest until Namibia is liberated than from a desire for individual revenge. When talking about the past, he struggled against the emotions that at times threatened to overwhelm us both, against the impact of memories he would rather bury but which must be preserved to tell the full story of colonial oppression. Only once or twice did I see a spark of personal hatred in his eyes as he related his treatment at the hands of the South African and PIDE butchers.

Throughout our work Nehova kept reminding me that there are still hundreds of his comrades who continue to suffer in the jails of the apartheid regime. It is to them that he has dedicated this story. (Recorded by Ole Gjerstad. Transcribed and edited by the collective effort of comrades at the LSM Information Center.)

Letter
From
Robben
Island

drawing by
Selma Waldman

Robben Island is a former leper colony in the icy currents off Cape Town. Thirteen hundred Black South African and Namibian prisoners are now incarcerated in its dungeons. Eight hundred of these are political prisoners, including SWAPO patriots such as Hermann Toivo ja Toivo and Elieser Tuhadeleni. This letter is reprinted from **Namibia News,** *September 1976.*

I am writing to you to tell you of our plight and to try to summarize the conditions prevailing at Robben Island, in the hope that you will be able to make these things known to the world. The South African regime spreads a lot of lies about this place, and we want you to broadcast the truth.

LABOR

We are forced to do the dirtiest and worst kinds of hard labor thought up by the Boers and designed to make life difficult and unbearable for us. For one year we were working at the "Bamboos" (it is a kind of seaweed) factory. Some of us were drawing the "Bamboos" from the sea, while others carried them to the factory. After they dry they are milled, put into bags, and exported to the United States, through San Francisco; to Japan, through Yokohama; and to France, through Marseilles. We were forced to produce up to 40 bags a day, each weighing 200 kg. We understand from a reliable source that these imperialist powers—who are now sucking the last drops of blood of the prisoners—are producing about 26 different products from these "Bamboos"—including jelly and perfume.

The factory where we were milling the "Bamboos" was full of dust from the machines. A doctor established that the dust is dangerous and injurious to the lungs and throat. The "equipment" we were given for protection against the dust was of the poorest quality, and didn't even serve its purpose. In November 1975 we decided to go on strike, since they had constructed an enclosure which was accessible to the dust coming from the machine and forced us to chop the "Bamboos" in that enclosure. The strike was successful in a sense, for they replaced us with common law prisoners, who have their jail about one kilometer from ours. Early this year the Boers tried us for this: they found us "guilty" and punished us.

Comrades also have to work on the lime quarry, which is about 80 meters long and 40–50 meters wide. Its depth is approximately 10–15 meters! The surface is hard like a stone, but we are forced, violently, to break it with picks. Often the lime is not needed, and they throw it into the sea. If you were to visit Robben Island and to see the lime quarries dug by human strength, you would certainly not believe your eyes. We also have to break stones, for gravel.

South Africa always tries to make visitors to the Island believe that hard labor does not exist there. They do this by concealing the existence of the quarries and wood camps; by giving those who work in these places other kinds of work to do whenever they have a visitor from abroad; and by giving deceptive explanations as to why people are working in such places.

MEDICAL TREATMENT

There is in fact a place called the "hospital" but is one only in name, for people do not get proper treatment there. The "doctors" who visit the Island are quacks: comrades are often given wrong tablets and medicines. Or the officers see to it that we don't get the tablets at all. We have put this matter on many occasions to the International Red Cross, but the Boers explain it away, and our complaints only intensify our maltreatment. Sometimes those who are ill and need urgently to be in hospital are put in isolation cells and receive no medical attention.

The following comrades lost their lives or parts of their bodies because they were not given proper medical attention by the Boer doctors:

Erasmus Kapolo had an abcess of the gum while in detention in Pretoria from 1966. The doctor extracted his tooth without anaesthetic, and when the abcess got worse and he asked for further treatment, he was given electric shock torture. A few days later, in 1967, he died.

Angula Shoonyeka was wounded during the capture at Ongulumbashe, but had recovered by the time he was taken to Pretoria. There the Security Police tortured and murdered him. They hung his body in his cell and said he had committed suicide. Two or three days before his death, on 9 October 1966, he told one of his comrades that he had been beaten and was going to be taken back to the torture chamber.

Festus Nehale had an incomplete rectum operation and was returned to the section only three days after the operation. The surgeon had not sewn him up properly, and comrade Nehale was so weak that the comrades had to wash him and support him. On 8 March 1970, a few days after the Boers had finally taken him to the local "hospital," comrade Nehale died.

Petrus Nilenge died on 4 March 1974, from TB. He had been taken to Cape Town for treatment, but returned in a worse condition. The back of his head swelled up, and he partly lost the power of speech. All the time until his death he was kept in isolation in the hospital—we were not allowed to see him. The Boers refused to admit for about 20 days after his death that he had died—they said they had released him.

John Shiponeni's knee was injured by the Boer torturers in Pretoria. One day on the Island he stumbled in the lime quarry and further damaged it. He was refused treatment for a month, then taken to Cape Town where his leg was amputated, without his knowledge or consent. They told him he had cancer and there was nothing they could do to save his leg. He now stays permanently in the "hospital."

Nghidipo Haufiki has high blood pressure; so does Sakeus Itika; Lazarus Sakaria has TB; Jonas Shimweefeleni has kidney trouble, the doctors have on numerous occasions recommended that he be released, but this request has been refused by the South African regime.

STUDY

Study on Robben Island is a privilege which the Boers may take away or suspend whenever it pleases them. Books are taken away from us soon after we receive them; those who take examinations never pass them, no matter how hard they work. It is very expensive to study—the greedy capitalist college owners are squeezing prisoners dry. There is a library, but we are only allowed to visit it at intervals of months, if at all. When we are sent books by the Red Cross or other international organizations, they simply do not reach us.

PUNISHMENTS

The comrades are punished every day by the Boers to destroy their psychological resistance. But brutality only helps to toughen the comrades. There is a "court" conducted by the Boer warders to punish us. If you are found "guilty," you are sent to isolation cells for 20 to 30 days, where you undergo a dietary punishment called "spare diet": for breakfast you get mealie-meal in hot water without salt; for lunch you get a beaker of soup without salt; dinner is the same as breakfast.

Maltreatment is an everyday thing. We are assaulted by warders and officers alike, then left in isolation cells until we no longer bear the marks, then taken to the hospital so the doctors can "prove" we have not been beaten. Sometimes they come and beat us up with handles in the night.

FOOD

The food is very unwholesome. For breakfast one gets porridge; for lunch—mealies; for dinner—porridge, with a tiny piece of meat or fish. "Coffee" is made from roasted mealie-meal and tastes terrible. Because of the poor food and brackish water, more than ¾ of the prisoners suffer from high blood pressure.

LETTERS AND VISITORS

We are allowed to write one letter a month, and receive one a month; if one has no visitor that month, one can write and receive two letters. The letters take months to reach us; they are censored and mutilated. Sometimes one only receives the name and address of the person who wrote the letter—the contents have been cut out. Our letters are also censored.

We are not allowed to have contact-visits, or even to shake hands with our visitors. We have to speak through a glass panel about 40 sq. cm., so that we cannot even see each other clearly. The visit lasts 30 minutes—once a month—and the Security Police are present and tape our conversations.

GENERAL

There are no beds—we have to sleep on hard sisal mats. Sometimes the cement is so cold that one cannot sleep and has to spend the night awake.

Comrades Ja Toivo, Mandela, Sisulu, and 37 other South Africans are kept in isolation in what the Boers call "single cells" (in order to deceive the international bodies which visit the Islands). They are very tiny.

On days when there is no work we are locked up the whole day and only given a few minutes outside the cells.

The Boers treat us here worse than they would treat dogs. They try to subdue and frighten us. But we are determined and resolved never to cringe before the Boers. We will continue to resist until the day of victory. We are prepared to be killed rather than to go over to the enemy's side.

Rumors have been circulating recently that comrade Ja Toivo and some others are to be released so that they can participate in the Turnhalle. This is only South African propaganda aimed at dividing our People's Movement. The Namibians on Robben Island have discussed this issue several times. One of our main decisions was that we will never talk to the South African regime because we are in prison and the South Africans are quite aware of the fact that we don't get any news about what is going on outside prison walls. We have no newspapers or radios. We also feel we have nothing to negotiate with the South African regime, since it was given the Mandate to administer Namibia without consultation with the Namibian people.

I feel that South Africa will only transfer us to Namibia when international pressure and the effect of our political and armed struggle have become unbearable—that is when South Africa will be completely defeated.

Reprinted from *Namibia News,* Vol. 9, No. 9, September 1976.

Political Program Of SWAPO

President Sam Nujoma
awards SWAPO militant - LSM photo

Newly recruited guerrillas
receive political orientation - MPLA photo

Introduction

The historical development of SWAPO up to the present time can be discussed in terms of four important stages and their respective tasks. First, the fundamental question which confronted the Namibian people during the latter half of the 1950's was the establishment of a political organization or a party which was capable of providing leadership and an organizational framework through which the spontaneous and scattered anti-colonial activities which characterized that period could be given an organizational expression. Prior to the formation of SWAPO, there were un-coordinated anti-colonial activities which were expressed in the form of localized strikes against colonial rule and individual petitionings to the United Nations concerning the South African racist oppression in Namibia. It was realized then that the establishment of a political organization was the most appropriate and effective way by which the politically conscious elements of our society could come into a direct and constant contact with the broad masses of our people to give articulate expression to the problems, aspirations and hopes of these masses. Thus SWAPO was formed on 19th April, 1960, as a concrete response to that fundamental need.

into exile. These initial measures of repression helped to underline two facts which were to prove basic to the development of the struggle in subsequent years:

(a) The Namibian people were made to realize the limitless nature of the South African brutality when it came to the defence of white supremacy; and

(b) SWAPO was obliged to take stock of the fact that only a political organization with firm roots in the broad masses of our society could weather the storm of repression and bring the liberation struggle to a successful conclusion.

Secondly, therefore, rooting SWAPO firmly in Namibian society came to be the main task during the early half of the 1960's. To this end, steps were taken to establish branches in different parts of the country, especially in the industrial areas of Windhoek, Otjiwarongo, Tsumeb, Walvis Bay, Luderitz Bay and Oranjemund.

Since the system of contract labor has been and continues to be one of the most blatant manifestations of colonial oppression and exploitation in Namibia, it was felt essential to initially root the movement in the workers' section of the population. This close historic identification of our movement with the interests of the toiling masses of the Namibian people is one of the main factors which ex-

96

plain the resilience of our movement when compared to other anti-colonial groups which had emerged in Namibia and have either collapsed or remained paper organizations.

The task of rooting the movement firmly in the society also entailed the concentration of the principal issues around which the masses had to be mobilized. This meant that SWAPO had to place the particularized problems, such as arbitrary residential relocation and contract labor, into the broader context of Namibia's national independence. This was the real beginning of the development of Namibian national consciousness. But since this trend of development represented a direct antithesis to South African colonialism in Namibia, it brought about new waves of repression against SWAPO. For instance, by December 1963 the South African government had banned all public meetings in Namibia. A score of SWAPO cadres came under severe harassment in the form of dismissals from jobs and schools, and expulsions from urban areas to the countryside. Concomitant with this stream of harassments, the South African government (early in 1964) set up a commission (known as the Odendaal Commission) to draw up a plan for the balkanization of Namibia into a chain of bantustans.

Thirdly, in the face of the above stated measures of repression, designed to thwart the growth of our movement, it became necessary to establish a guerrilla network of which the People's Liberation Army of Namibia (PLAN)—SWAPO's military wing—is today the living expression. The consolidation of PLAN, in the face of the enemy's concerted effort to wipe out this guerrilla force while it was in its infancy, became crucial during the latter half of the 1960's. The basic problem was the horrendous demand imposed on PLAN to overcome the enemy's strategic plan to cut off our eastern logistic network linking our fighting units inside the country and the supplying rear-base—independent Africa.

While the enemy was tightening his grip on the internal activities of SWAPO, following the initial encounter in 1966 between our combatants and South African troops, the leadership abroad called a Consultative Congress of SWAPO during the months of December and January 1969/70 to plan a strategy and program of action for an intensified armed and political struggle. To achieve this objective the organizational structure of the Party was broadened by creating new departments, e.g. Labor, Women, Youth, etc., for the political mobilization of the people of Namibia in masses. Other departments like that of Defence were reactivated to meet the demands of intensified armed struggle.

The immediate effect of this program was manifested in the growing militancy of the Namibian populace as demonstrated by the historic 1971/72 general strike of workers as well as by the militant activities of the SWAPO Youth League.

Fourthly, the first half of the 1970's has seen armed liberation struggle becoming the main form of SWAPO's campaign to bring about genuine and total independence for the people of Namibia.

In summary, it can be said that the roots of the contemporary Namibian national liberation movement can be traced to the formation of political organization during the latter half of the 1950's.

The year 1960 saw the formation of SWAPO. The first half of the 1960's witnessed the dynamic development of the movement, characterized by the consolidation of SWAPO in Namibian society and the establishment of the People's liberation Army of Namibia. During the latter half of the 1960's the movement had to strengthen itsguerrilla infrastructure in the face of the enemy's harsh counter-revolutionary measures. The early part of the 1970's was marked by the application of the Tanga strategy of intensified political and military struggle.

In the present phase, armed struggle has become the main form of SWAPO's resistance to South Africa's racist, oppressive and exploitative occupation of Namibia.

The defeat of fascist rule in Portugal in April 1974 brought a new dimension to the Namibian liberation struggle. It has made it possible for thousands of our people to move across the Angola/Namibian frontiers to the rear bases of our struggle to obtain both the skills and tools of armed struggle. Hence, thousands of workers, peasants and patriotic intellectuals have been enlisting in PLAN since the early half of 1974.

Present and Future Tasks

The tasks before SWAPO at present and in the immediate future are:

a) The liberation and winning of independence for the people of Namibia, by all possible means, and the establishment of a democratic people's government; and

b) The realization of genuine and total independence of Namibia in the spheres of politics, economy, defence, social and cultural affairs.

To these ends, SWAPO has resolved:

a) To persistently mobilize and organize the broad masses of the

Namibian people so that they can actively participate in the national liberation struggle.

b) To mold and strengthen, in the thick of the national liberation struggle, the bond of national and political consciousness amongst the Namibian people.

c) To combat all manifestations and tendencies of tribalism, regionalism, ethnic orientation and racial discrimination.

d) To unite all Namibian people, particularly the working class, the peasantry and progressive intellectuals, into a vanguard party capable of safeguarding national independence and of building a classless, nonexploitative society based on the ideals and principles of scientific socialism.

SWAPO Foreign Policy

1. SWAPO holds high the banner of international anti-imperialist solidarity. In pursuance of anti-imperialist solidarity, the movement has resolved:

a) To work in solidarity with other national liberation movements and other anti-imperialist, progressive and peace-loving forces throughout the world with a view to ridding Namibia, the African continent and mankind of colonialist and imperialist domination;

b) To support and promote the ideals of unity of Africa as provided for in the Charter of the Organization of African Unity (OAU);

c) To work in close cooperation with all progressive governments, organizations and popular forces for the total emancipation of the African continent;

d) To fight against all maneuvers from any quarter that are aimed at a reactionary solution which is contrary to the realization of a total and genuine liberation of Namibia; and

e) To foster and strengthen anti-imperialist unity amongst the national liberation, world socialist, progressive and peace-loving forces in order to eliminate all forms of imperialism, colonialism and neocolonialism.

2. The Foreign Relations Secretariat of SWAPO is urged to streamline our foreign missions in different parts of the world for an intensified diplomatic offensive aimed at exposing the current South African colonial maneuvers designed to impose a puppet confederation of Bantustans on our people. This offensive is to be carried out along the following lines:

a) strive for comprehensive publicity of the fact that the South African puppets, now gathering at the Turnhalle circus, have no mandate or support from the Namibian population for their collaborationist role;

b) expose the attempts by certain Western governments to give international publicity to the Turnhalle puppets by extending invitations to these puppets and by giving publicity to the puppets' treacherous views on radio, television and in the press; it must be made clear that this publicity is being orchestrated behind the scenes by the South African government and its big business public relations lobby—the South African Foundation;

c) strengthen our anti-imperialist international solidarity with the socialist countries, working-class movements of the capitalist countries, liberation support organizations, and friendly governments and ordinary people;

d) heighten the campaign to isolate South Africa from every possible source of support, comfort or contact with the rest of the world, because of its illegal occupation of Namibia and its institutionalized race oppression at home;

e) this heightening campaign is aimed at the following aspects of international contacts:
   (1) financial and commercial;
   (2) professional and sporting;
   (3) cultural and academic; and
   (4) diplomatic and tourist.

f) make it abundantly clear to the world that SWAPO will never stop the armed and political struggle until Pretoria meets the following preconditions:
   (1) South Africa must publically accept the right of the Namibian people to independence and national sovereignty.
   (2) South Africa must publicly announce that Namibian territorial integrity is absolute and not negotiable in any quarter.
   (3) All political prisoners must be released including Hermann ya Toivo and many other leaders and colleagues on Robben Island and elsewhere.
   (4) All political exiles, of whatever political organization, must be allowed freely to return to their country without fear of arrest or victimization.
   (5) South Africa must commit herself to the removal of her police and army and stop using Namibia as a base for aggression against neighboring, independent African countries.

(6) Any constitutional talks on the future of Namibia must take place under United Nations supervision, and should aim at the holding of free elections in Namibia under United Nations supervision and control.

g) reiterate our stand that SWAPO shall under no circumstances accept the South African plan to impose on our people a weak and fearful confederation of Bantustans, a confederation which will be incapable of contradicting neocolonial orders from Pretoria.

Internal Political Guidelines

1. To achieve the aims and objectives of SWAPO and to implement its revolutionary political line, all sections and organs of the organization are charged with the immediate task of disseminating the Constitution and policy documents to the broad masses of the Namibian people.

2. All sections and organs of SWAPO are called upon to make supreme efforts towards the building of a reliable core of leading cadres who are capable of being in close and constant touch with the people at all levels. This task is to be accomplished in the following ways:

a) strive to raise the political consciousness of the cadres through regular discussion groups in the local community; the discussions must aim at imparting a fundamental knowledge of the concrete political reality in Namibia and the world revolutionary process; and

b) the more politically conscious cadres in each section and organ are urged to put themselves in direct contact with the comrades who are less acquainted with the complex issues of national and social liberation.

3. The cadres have the immediate and imperative duty to rally the broad masses of the Namibian people against the occupation regime. This programmatic directive is to be carried out in the following manner:

a) each cadre must link himself or herself in a fundamental way to the inarticulate, largely illiterate toiling masses of our people; learn from them about their true aspirations, their problems, their doubts and their sense of possibilities;

b) the cadres must then sum up the ideas of the masses in terms of their own wider experience and sense of responsibility;

c) they must then return these ideas to the masses in an articulate form and pose new questions with a view to deepening the political understanding of the masses and help them to overcome their inarticulateness, their suspicions of change and their ignorance of modern organizational possibilities; and

d) by the method of political work, SWAPO shall involve the whole population in active discussion; which is the main precondition for the people's explicit and conscious commitment to the policy of the movement.

Armed Struggle

SWAPO holds the conviction that armed resistance to the South African occupation in our country is the only viable and effective means left for us to achieve genuine liberation in Namibia.

However, much as we are convinced that armed struggle must now be the main form of our liberation activity, we do not beautify war or regard it as a form of sport. We see war for what it really is—an extension of politics by other means. It is the continuation of political relations in the form of violence.

But as in all other political relations, in examining any war, one must seek to understand the nature of the politics being pursued. As social relations, political acts are either just or unjust and just political acts are naturally to be supported. Hence, a clear distinction between the war of justice and wars of injustice must always be made. We consider our own armed liberation struggle as just, and, therefore, deserving support from all justice and peace-loving peoples. In supporting or committing oneself to the winning of victory by the oppressed peoples or nations, one is helping to bring about conditions under which war will be ended forever. For where there is oppression, there will always be armed resistance to bring about justice. It is in this light that we appeal for world support in our war of liberation.

In our struggle to bring justice to the oppressed people of Namibia, SWAPO is working towards a universal arming of the people, that is, to transform the armed struggle in Namibia into a truly people's war. The necessary political mobilization to implement this vital aspect of our program is already in motion.

In pursuance of this strategic objective, the following measures are being undertaken:

a) All cadres of PLAN are exhorted to uphold the supremacy of the Organization over all its sections;

b) All commanding cadres of the People's Liberation Army of Namibia are called upon to make concrete efforts towards correctly grasping the revolutionary role of the masses in the struggle and to recognize that this role is the primary condition for victory;

c) These cadres are not only to lead the war but also to assist in propagating SWAPO's political line among the people in all the zones of combat;

d) New zones of combat must be constantly opened up in application of the strategy of active attacks on the enemy at many places at the same time in order for PLAN to maintain and extend its control of the battlefield; and

e) Political education in the people's armed forces must at all times be deep-going, since it is the most vital precondition for bringing about a steeled revolutionary discipline among the combatants.

Economic Reconstruction

Colonized Namibia has two economies:

a) A wealthy white-owned economy based on the extensive extraction of the country's varied natural resources; and

b) A separate subsistence economy enveloping the majority of the African population who are forced to live in Bantustans.

The two economies have been consciously designed in accordance with the social interests of the white settler group and international monopoly capitalism.

The African masses have been forced to live in impoverished Bantustans. They are being held in these Bantustans as labor hostages, because in order for them to survive, they must of necessity seek employment as cheap laborers in the white-controlled mining, fishing and ranching industries.

The colonialists argue falsely that Namibia does not have agricultural potential. Their strategy has been to prevent commercial farming in Namibia so that the country depends on the agricultural products of South Africa. That is to say, Namibia has been consciously reduced to a captive market, a dumping ground of South Africa's own agricultural industry.

A nation which is dependent on another country for the food consumption of its population cannot be but a hostage of the particular country which feeds its population.

A close analysis of Namibia's agricultural potential shows that the northern/central areas of Namibia are quite capable of producing more than sufficient food to feed the entire Namibian population, provided that a conscious policy is adopted to engage a considerable number of the working masses in this particular field of production.

In a SWAPO-governed Namibia, the state shall take keen interest in providing adequate, modern tools and instruments for large scale agricultural production, with a view to making the country agriculturally self-reliant.

The colonial regime in our country has been interested not only in making Namibia a captive market of South Africa's agricultural industry, but also in concentrating African labor in the extensive extraction of Namibia's mineral resources with a view to taking out as much of our resources as possible in the shortest possible time.

The other negative consequence of this colonial strategy has been the conscious effort to prevent Namibia from developing processing industries. Thus, the huge bulk of the finished products in Namibia comes from South Africa. In this respect, Namibia is again used as a dumping ground for the products of South African factories.

Thus the economic reconstruction in a free, democratic and united Namibia will have as its motive force the establishment of a classless society. Social justice and progress for all is the governing idea behind every SWAPO policy decision. The government of a truly liberated Namibia will, therefore, be called upon to take the following measures:

a) Wage the struggle towards the abolition of all forms of exploitation of man by man and destructive spirit of individualism and aggrandizement of wealth and power by individuals, groups or classes.

b) Ensure that all the major means of production and exchange of the country are owned by the people.

c) Strive for the creation of an integrated national economy in which there is a proper balance between agricultural and industrial development along the following lines:

(1) the establishment of processing industry;

(2) a comprehensive agrarian reform aimed at giving land to the tillers;

(3) the establishment of peasants' or farmers' cooperatives or collectives;

(4) the establishment of state-owned ranching and crop farms, aimed at making Namibia an agriculturally self-sufficient nation, and

(5) the cultivation of a spirit of self-reliance among our people.

Education and Culture

A deep-going socio-economic transformation of Namibian society depends upon the speedy development of the Namibian productive forces, particularly the development of the skills, knowledge and cultural creativeness of the toiling masses. Hence, our movement is called upon to embark on:

a) urgent training of technical and professional cadres at institutions of technical and higher learning in different parts of the world as well as the newly established United Nations Institute for Namibia.

b) provision for work-oriented functional literacy, that is, comprehensive education and training for illiterate and semi-literate adults (with a literacy component built in) at SWAPO schools.

c) laying the foundation of a free universal education for all Namibians from primary through secondary to university level by training many teachers and educators now.

d) developing the people's cultural creativeness as a weapon in the struggle for liberation.

e) the sufferings and aspirations of the masses must be the central themes of all our artistic expressions; namely, drawings, music, paintings, dancing, literature, etc.

f) we must strive toward the elimination of all the vestiges of tribal or feudal mentality, particularly the unscientific or superstitious conceptions of natural and social phenomena.

Health and Social Services

1. At present, the Health and Social Welfare Secretariat of the Movement is called upon to strengthen our existing clinics in the rear bases as well as our mobile clinics in the operational zones and to set up new ones.

2. Our health and social services program in an independent Namibia shall strive for preventive as well as curative medicine for all citizens, along the following lines:

a) there shall be comprehensive, free medical services in an independent and democratic Namibia;

b) there shall be hospitals and clinics in every district of our country;

c) there shall be nurseries and clinics in every community for the working people and their families;

d) there shall be health education centers for preventive medicine and family planning;

e) there shall be institutions for training medical and para-medical personnel;

f) there shall be rehabilitation Centers for disabled and infirm persons, and

g) there shall be an International Red Cross Society.

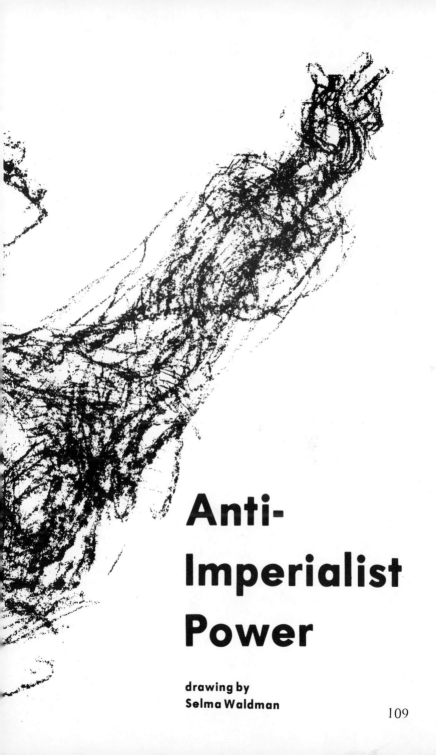

Anti-Imperialist Power

drawing by
Selma Waldman

109

This article first appeared in **Namibia**, *the official organ of SWAPO,*
Volume 1, Number 1, 1977.

There are many slogans to be written on the banner of international anti-imperialist solidarity. What is written there will eventually determine along which road it is carried. When the slogans are written there is no substitute for clarity. Marching beneath this banner we must know our enemy.

So—what is imperialism? How do we understand it? How is it destroyed?

Despite the internationalization of capitalist relations, the great monopolies are still rooted in national economic formations.

To take up the challenge of the call for anti-imperialist solidarity we must first be clear on the nature of imperialism. It is not enough to view it simply, as some do, as a *policy* pursued by states and/or business interests within the advanced industrial powers, and thus to imply that the goal of the national liberation movements in eliminating imperialism is the achievement of a shift in the policy of the businesses or governments concerned.

Imperialism is a world system. It divides the world into oppressed and oppressor nations. Its form is not a chance one. It is a stage in the development of the world capitalist economic system. It is the stage of monopolies—of the concentration of capital in fewer and fewer hands. According to Lenin it is the highest, or final, stage of capitalism; a transitional stage which opens up the road to socialism.*

Historically, the culmination of the colonial expansion of the nineteenth century, which was marked by the incorporation of the whole world into the system of capitalist relations, coincided with the emergence of monopoly as the dominant form of capital. The history of imperialism has been characterized by the struggle between monopolies to divide and redivide the world between themselves. This has taken and still takes the form of struggles between nations; for despite the internationalization of capitalist relations, the great monopolies are still rooted in national economic formations. Imperialism is characterized by the competition between national monopolies for access to spheres of economic activity which, by their relative underdevelopment, guarantee a higher than average rate of profit. Namibia is a case in point.

---

* V.I. Lenin, *Imperialism, the Highest State of Capitalism.*

The colonization of Namibia brought with it the incorporation of economic and trading relations into the capitalist economic system of the western world. The gross exploitation of Namibian labor and minerals and other raw materials which ensued has underdeveloped the economy and has benefitted the colonial powers—first Germany, then South Africa—and international capitalism as a whole. The role that South Africa has played as a colonial power has been to develop the system of apartheid as a specific framework for capitalist exploitation. Apartheid in South Africa and Namibia has created the conditions for massive profits and the world's second highest rate of return for both South African and Western investment.

In other countries, however, imperialism operates within different frameworks. It has demonstrated clearly that it is not tied to, and cannot be identified with, any one form of political domination of the oppressed by the oppressor nation.

This is borne out by the process of decolonization of Africa which has taken place over the last fifteen years. Decolonization has meant the removal of the direct political/military representatives of the colonial powers, and has led to a variety of forms of "self-determination." However, in the majority of cases there has been no real obstacle to the continued exploitation of those countries by international capital. Economic independence has not come automatically with the gaining of the political kingdom; most former colonies are still embedded in the imperialist structure.

There are no enemy races or peoples. The enemy of our people is that of all peoples: colonialism which has no race, imperialism which has no country.

Samora Machel, 1973

We have much to learn from the experiences of those former colonies who now have political independence and who are fighting to overcome the ways in which their economies have been underdeveloped to benefit imperialism. The strategy most widely evolved in Africa and in other parts of the Third World has been to use state power for the expropriation of at least part of the most important industries. It consists of using those industries where a relatively high degree of accumulation of capital has occurred as a basis for establishing a competitive trading position vis-a-vis the imperialist powers. Where it can fail is in not taking into account the sheer extent of the discrepancy between the economic development of imperialist nations and the former colonies. Moreover, where the state is allied with an incipient local capitalist class it can lead to its opposition to "big capital" on behalf of the smaller and developing local capital, and can thus merely serve the interests of the local bourgeoisie. To avoid this it is essential therefore to identify and understand the class forces united in the national liberation struggles still in progress. This lesson is contained in many of the writings of Amilcar Cabral.

The lesson to learn from Mozambique and Angola, as from Cambodia and Viet Nam, is that the people's struggle can win even against the mightiest military powers. But this lesson must be carefully understood, and we must claim no easy victories. The interests of imperialism will not always be best served by the continuation of direct political/military control, and we must guard against assuming that a military defeat of imperialist powers is a defeat for imperialism itself. South Africa's foreign policy provides a clear and useful example.

South Africa has taken the line of detente, whereas with Angola it took the line of direct military invasion.

It appears to comprise two contradictory elements: detente and military intervention. Since 1969 South Africa has developed an "outward-looking" policy of detente towards the rest of Southern Africa and of Africa as a whole. This extends to Latin America and other parts of the Third World and is intimately bound up with the need for economic expansion. This has not meant an end to South Africa's military intervention in the subcontinent and acts of aggression against neighboring independent countries. In practice, detente and military intervention are two facets of the same policy. They are both expressions of imperialism and are both working to promote the interests of imperialism. In the case of Zimbabwe and Mozambique, South Africa has taken the line of detente, whereas with Angola it took the line of direct military invasion and continuing military attacks once its invasion was thwarted. In Zimbabwe, Vorster is prepared to push Ian Smith to hand over power because he would rather see the country become a client-state with a pliable black government representing the local incipient bourgeoisie. With Mozambique, Vorster is at the moment prepared to live in "peaceful co-existence" because of the extent to which Mozambique's economy has been historically integrated into South Africa's. South Africa is, of course, also remarkably dependent on the flow of Mozambican workers to the mines in the Transvaal.

Angola's economy, which is potentially much wealthier than Mozambique's, has never been significantly integrated into South Africa's. South Africa's plans for a capitalist Southern Africa Common Market, and for ever-increasing economic links within the subcontinent, necessitates the incorporation of the Angolan economy. Thus its invasion of Angola was a desperate attempt by South Africa to guarantee its interests by seizing the opportunity of allying itself with counter-revolutionary forces in Angola.

The Western powers are looking for a "Solution" which will interrupt the political mobilization of the Namibian masses.

The direction in which South Africa will move on Namibia still hangs in the balance. It is obviously in its interests that Namibia remains firmly within the imperialist economic system, and this would be best assured by a neocolonial solution in Namibia. The concern of the imperialist powers themselves to ensure this development can be seen very clearly in the March 1977 United States State Department/AID study on Namibia and Zimbabwe which stresses the need to ensure the safety of US economic interests and political and strategic presence in Southern Africa as a whole.

Western objections to the Turnhalle are based on the fact that they recognize it would have led to an intensified armed struggle and a more violent transition to independence. The western powers are looking for a "solution" which will interrupt the political mobilization of the Namibian masses, because this mobilization threatens the establishment of class alliances favorable to imperialism.

As long as South Africa remains a bulwark of capitalism, the independence of the rest of the subcontinent is going to be continually threatened. The key role that South Africa plays for imperialism in the subcontinent means that the liberation of Namibia and Zimbabwe, and the consolidation of socialism in Mozambique and Angola, is dependent on the revolution in South Africa itself. Given our understanding of imperialism as a world system, it is not sufficient to break the hold of South Africa over the subcontinent.

To open the path to true liberation we must break imperialism as a world economic system. It is thus that we can fully understand the directive of SWAPO's Political Program in saying that we must "strengthen our anti-imperialist solidarity with the socialist countries, working class movements of the capitalist countries, liberation support organizations ..."

The other lesson to learn from the liberation struggles in Mozambique and Angola is a lesson of international anti-imperialist action. For the first time in the history of colonial wars, workers of the colonial power, Portugal, launched an armed struggle against the colonial war machine in their fight to break the Salazar-Caetano regime and to end the oppression they suffered at its hands. The ruling classes of the imperialist powers can no longer afford to become tied down in large-scale colonial wars in their dependent peripheries for an extended period or they will face the immediate threat of collapse at the center—at home.

The concrete conditions exist for building an anti-imperialist movement which links the struggle and interests of workers of all nations in solidarity against the common enemy—international capitalism.

It is sufficient to recall that in our present historical situation— elimination of imperialism which uses every means to perpetuate its domination over our people and consolidation of socialism throughout a large part of the world—there are only two possible paths for an independent nation: to return to imperialist domination (neo-colonialism, capitalism, state capitalism) or take the path of socialism.

Amilcar Cabral

SWAPO
Constitution

Definition

SWAPO is a national liberation movement rallying together, on the basis of free and voluntary association, all freedom-inspired sons and daughters of the Namibian people. It is the organized political vanguard of the oppressed and exploited people of Namibia. In fulfilling its vanguard role, SWAPO organizes, unites, inspires, orients and leads the broad masses of working Namibian people in the struggle for national and social liberation. It is thus the expression and embodiment of national unity, of a whole people united and organized in the struggle for total independence and social liberation.

AIMS AND OBJECTIVES

A. Preamble

1) Whereas Namibia is still under foreign domination;
2) Whereas the Namibian people's unalienable and imprescriptable right to self-determination and national independence is denied;
3) Whereas the occupying colonial power persists in its refusal to unconditionally withdraw all its repressive military and police forces and its administration from Namibia.
4) Whereas the occupying regime persists in its efforts to consolidate its illegal occupation by intensified repression and the fragmentation of Namibia into bantustans; and
5) Whereas the regime continues to disregard the Namibian people's deep yearning for freedom;

B. Now, Therefore Do Declare
the Basic Aims and Objectives of SWAPO as Follows:

1) To fight relentlessly for the immediate and total liberation of Namibia from colonial and imperialist occupation;

2) To unite all the people of Namibia, irrespective of race, religion, sex or ethnic origin, into a cohesive, representative, national political entity;

3) To foster a spirit of national consciousness or a sense of common purpose and collective destiny among the people of Namibia;

4) To combat all reactionary tendencies of individualism, tribalism, racism, sexism and regionalism;

5) To cooperate to the fullest extent with all the genuine national liberation movements, organizations and individuals throughout the world towards complete elimination of the colonial system of imperialism;

6) To establish in Namibia a democratic and secular government founded upon the will and participation of all the Namibian people;

7) To ensure that the people's government exercises effective control over the means of production and distribution and pursues a policy which facilitates the way to social ownership of all the resources of the country;

8) To work towards the creation of a non-exploitative and non-oppressive classless society;

9) To ensure that a people's government in an independent Namibia cooperates with other states in Africa in bringing about African unity;

10) To see that the people's government works in close cooperation with all peace-loving states towards world peace and security.

Membership

Membership of SWAPO shall be open to every Namibian who accepts the aims and objectives as set out above.

Selected Readings

COURTNEY, Winnifred and Jennifer DAVIS. *Namibia: US Corporate Involvement*. New York: The Africa Fund, 1972. 32 pp. (Order from ACOA, 305 East 46th Street, New York, NY 10017)

FIRST, Ruth. *South West Africa*. Harmondsworth: Penguin, 1963.

FIRST, Ruth and Ronald SEGAL (eds.). *South West Africa: A Travesty of Trust*. London: Andre Deutsch, 1967.

FRAENKEL, Peter. *The Namibians of South West Africa*. London: Minority Rights Group, 1974. 48 pp. (Order from MRG, 36 Craven Street, London WC2N 5NG)

MURRAY, Roger et al. *The Role of Foreign Firms in Namibia*. London: Africa Publications Trust, 1974. 220 pp. (Order from APT, 48 Grafton Way, London WIP 5LB)

NDADI, Vinnia (edited by Dennis Mercer). *Breaking Contract: the Story of Vinnia Ndadi*. Richmond, Canada: LSM Press, 1974. 116 pp. (Order from LSM Information Center, PO Box 2077, Oakland, CA 94604, USA)

SWAPO of Namibia. *Namibia*. (Official organ of SWAPO) (Order from SWAPO of Namibia, Department of Information, 21/25 Tabernacle Street, London EC2 or from LSM, PO Box 2077, Oakland, CA 94604, USA)

Southern Africa Committee. *Southern Africa*. (Monthly magazine with regular section on Namibia) (Order from SAC, 156 Fifth Avenue, New York, NY 10010)

United Nations Information Service. *Namibia: A Trust Betrayed*. New York: UN Information Service, 1975. (Order from UN Information Service, UN Plaza, New York, NY 10017. This office will also furnish a list of UN documents on Namibia.)

VIGNE, Randolf. *A Dwelling Place of Our Own: The Story of the Namibian Nation*. London: International Defense and Aid Fund, 1975. 52 pp. (Order from IDAF, 104 Newgate Street, London EC1)

Actions

Namibia's new
generation:
their country
will be free !
- LSM photo

The first step toward building a stronger solidarity movement with SWAPO and the people of Namibia is that of providing information. Every year, the South African regime spends millions of dollars for newspaper ads and Madison Avenue promoters to put its "case" to the American public. Neither SWAPO nor the solidarity movement can match South Africa's resources. But a good beginning is to use this book or any of the materials listed on the previous page as a basis to mobilize your constituency, whether a school class, church group, union local, or political organization.

A second possibility is to invite a SWAPO representative to your city. To arrange this you can contact the New York SWAPO office (see address below).

The US government and large corporations play an important political and economic role in propping up the apartheid regime and South Africa's occupation of Namibia. By attacking these links, North Americans can help strangle the racist system. For example, American banks hold $2.2 billion in outstanding loans to South Africa; several organizations are now pressuring these banks to cut off their links with apartheid. At the same time, student, labor, and church committees are working to have their institutions withdraw all investment with American companies that operate in South Africa.

Campaigns to stop US support for the South African system can be combined with raising concrete support for SWAPO. The liberation movement is always short of means to implement all its programs; to get medicines, school material, and means of transport it has to turn to supporters abroad. Liberation Support Movement is currently raising funds to provide SWAPO with a self-sufficient printshop—a project which relies on support from people throughout this country. Other groups carry out similar support projects which depend on popular participation.

For more information on solidarity work with the Namibian liberation struggle, you can contact any of the groups and offices listed below.

United States

Liberation Support Movement, P.O. Box 2077, Oakland, CA 94604

American Committee on Africa, 305 E. 46th Street, New York, NY 10017

Chicago Committee for African Liberation, 1476 W. Irving Park Rd., Chicago, IL 60613

Bay Area Namibia Action Group, 944 Market Street, #308, San Francisco, CA 94101

United Nations Commissioner on Namibia, UN Plaza, New York, NY 10017

International Campaign Against Racism in Sport (Dennis Brutus), 624 Clark St., Evanston, IL 60201

Canada

Toronto Committee for the Liberation of Southern African Colonies, 121 Avenue Road, Toronto, Ontario

United Kingdom

Namibia Support Group, 21–25 Tabernacle Street, London EC2

SWAPO Offices

SWAPO Mission to the UN, 801 Second Avenue, Rm. 1401, New York, NY 10017

SWAPO, 21–25 Tabernacle Street, London, EC2, United Kingdom

SWAPO, Karduansmakargatan 4, S-111 52, Stockholm, Sweden

About
LSM

Liberation Support Movement is an independent anti-imperialist organization founded in 1968 and based in the United States and Canada. Through our Information Center we carry out educational work to help increase the internationalist consciousness of progressive Americans and build concrete links of solidarity with African and Asian liberation movements. Over the years we have published a wide range of literature and audio-visual documentation—from firsthand accounts by our own members to guerrilla autobiographies and interviews with movement leaders. At present, we are working to develop our quarterly journal, *LSM News,* as an instrument of analysis on national liberation struggles and developments in the anti-imperialist movement. By regularly touring the continent with these materials, LSM encourages others to themselves engage in active solidarity work—to turn their anti-imperialist sentiments into direct action.

In this way, our educational work also enables us to generate material support for liberation movements. With the participation of other groups and individuals, LSM has sent quantities of clothing, concentrated food, medical supplies, textbooks, and technical training and equipment to MPLA, FRELIMO, PAIGC, SWAPO of Namibia, and PFLO of Oman. Our current (1978) project is to supply SWAPO with equipment and training for a complete printshop in Africa. Your financial contribution is needed!

Our work represents but a small part of what North Americans can do to advance the struggle against US-dominated imperialism all over the world. In the absence of mass-based revolutionary organizations within the capitalist centers, the struggles of peasants and workers in the underdeveloped countries are the driving force of contemporary history. By actively supporting the movements that lead this fight, we help undermine the economic and military foundations of monopoly capitalism, accelerating a process that will ultimately culminate in the socialist transformation of North America, as well. The liberation of nations such as Zimbabwe, Namibia, and South Africa is in our own long-term interest; we must recognize and act upon the practical consequences of this!

We invite collaboration with progressive people within North America and overseas. Please write for a free catalog and information on our activities and let us hear about the work you are doing.

Subscribe to LSM NEWS

More on Namibia
from LSM Press...

Breaking Contract

Autobiography of
Vinnia Ndadi

For sixteen years a contract laborer and political activist in Namibia, Ndadi is now a member of SWAPO's National Executive. His story documents the successful efforts to organize migrant workers for national liberation and firmly establishes—through personal experience—the futility of "non-violent" strategies for social change in Namibia.
1974. 116 pp., drawings, maps $2⁴⁵

Poster for a Free Namibia

This beautiful poster in SWAPO's colors (red, blue, green) is a striking salute to the Namibian struggle for independence from South Africa. Designed by Art Works and printed by Glad Day Press as their contribution to the SWAPO Printshop Project. All proceeds go toward building a fully-equipped and staffed printshop for SWAPO in Africa.
17"x22" $1⁰⁰

Add 10% Postage & Handling to All Orders (50¢ Minimum)

2 88
0325